Russia's 1996 Presidential Election

Russia's 1996 Presidential Election

The End of Polarized Politics

Michael McFaul

Hoover Institution Press
Stanford University
Stanford, California

Hoover Institution Press Publication 442

Cover photo credits:
photo of Boris Yeltsin © 1996 H. J. Burkard/Bilderberg/Aurora;
photo of Gennadii Zyuganov courtesy of Hoover Institution Archives

First printing, 1997
03 02 01 00 99 98 97   9 8 7 6 5 4 3 2 1

Manufactured in the United States of America.

The paper used in this publication meets the minimum requirements
of American National Standard for Information Sciences—Permanence
of Paper for Printed Library Materials, ANSI Z39.48-1984. ⊛

Library of Congress Cataloging-in-Publication Data

McFaul, Michael, 1963–
    Russia's 1996 presidential election : the end of polarized politics /
Michael McFaul.
        p.   cm. — (Hoover Institution Press publication ; 442)
    Includes bibliographical references (p.   ) and index.
    ISBN 0-8179-9502-1 (pbk. : alk. paper)
    1. Presidents—Russia (Federation)—Election. 2. Elections—
Russia (Federation)—History. 3. Russia (Federation)—Politics and
government—1991– . I. Title. II. Series.
JN6699.A5M344   1997
324.947′086—dc21   97-9350
                                                            CIP

Contents

Preface

The 1996 presidential election represents a truly momentous event in Russian history. For the first time in a thousand years, Russian citizens selected their head of state in a democratic election. This volume examines and explains this event in detail. The first part highlights contextual and institutional factors influencing voter preferences. The second part traces the dynamics of the electoral campaigns of all major candidates, focusing in particular on incumbent Boris Yeltsin and challenger Gennadii Zyuganov. The final part of the volume discusses the implications of this election for democratic consolidation in Russia.

Much of the research for this volume was completed while I was working as a senior associate for the Carnegie Endowment of International Peace and based at the Moscow Carnegie Center, to which I continue to hold an affiliation. I am indebted to the Carnegie Endowment for International Peace and the Carnegie Corporation of New York for their general support of our electoral project at the Moscow Carnegie Center. I completed writing this volume at Stanford University. I am indebted to the Hoover Institution for assistance in the completion of this project, which is part of Hoover's Program on Democracy and Free Markets.

I would like to thank several people who have commented on or read drafts of this essay, including Vladimir Bokser, George Breslauer,

Larry Diamond, John Dunlop, Sergei Markov, Donna Norton, and Nikolai Petrov. Tanya Kovalenko and Tracey Sharon Jones provided valuable research assistance. I also am indebted to dozens of campaign officials from the Yeltsin, Zyuganov, Lebed, Yavlinsky, Zhirinovsky, and Gorbachev campaigns who generously gave me their time during a hectic period. In particular, I would like to thank Aleksandr Oslon, director of the Foundation for Public Opinion and the chief pollster for the Yeltsin campaign, for sharing with me some of his invaluable polling data from the Yeltsin campaign.[1] I also would like to thank Michael Specter and Alessandra Stanley from the *New York Times* and Lee Hockstader and David Hoffman from the *Washington Post* who shared with me polling data, campaign gossip, and professional insights during the election period.

Introduction

In January 1996, few analysts or politicians predicted that Boris Yeltsin would win reelection as Russia's president. In elections for parliament in December 1995, the Communist Party of the Russian Federation (CPRF) captured 22 percent of the popular vote, followed by ultra-nationalist Vladimir Zhirinovsky, whose Liberal Democratic Party of Russia (LDPR) won 11 percent. Our Home Is Russia, the proreformist electoral bloc founded by Prime Minister Viktor Chernomyrdin, won only 10 percent of the popular vote, while Grigorii Yavlinsky's Yabloko Party collected a paltry 7 percent. Most observers agreed with Peter Reddaway's assessment of the December 1995 electoral outcome.

> The results show unambiguously that hard-line forces made big gains; that democratic parties suffered heavy losses; that forces hostile to market reform advanced; and that both President Yeltsin and Prime Minister Chernomyrdin were humiliated.[1]

Stephen Cohen went even further when he argued that "90 percent of the electorate voted against Yeltsinism in December."[2] The logical conclusion of such interpretations of Russian electoral politics was that Yeltsin would surely lose a free and fair election in June 1996. As Daniel Singer reported, writing in *The Nation* in April 1996:

Indeed, the striking feature of the parliamentary elections last December was the overwhelming rejection of the politicians connected with the so-called shock therapy prescribed by the International Monetary Fund and practiced for the past four years. The odds are that they will vote in June in the same fashion. Not only is Zyuganov well ahead of the pack in all opinion polls, which show him capturing between 15 and 25 percent of the vote, but Yeltsin is quite often last in a bunch that hovers around 10 percent.[3]

Gennadii Zyuganov, the Communist Party presidential candidate, seemed assured of victory. Claiming that "the Communists are much closer to the mainstream of public opinion," three prominent scholars of Russian electoral politics—Evelyn Davidheiser, Jerry Hough, and Susan Lehman—concluded that "the Communists look to be in a very strong position for the 1996 election if they run a strong campaign and face a weak candidate such as Yeltsin."[4] In fact, the outcome of a free and fair election seemed so obvious that many predicted Yeltsin would either falsify the results or postpone the election entirely.[5] Several of his advisers urged him to do so.

History also appeared to be against Boris Yeltsin.[6] Throughout Eastern Europe, anticommunist leaders who won electoral victories in first elections lost to former communist leaders in second elections.[7] Even in the Czech Republic, Vaclav Klaus and his allies failed to win enough seats to reconstitute their old right-of-center coalition government.[8] Sali Berisha, president of Albania, managed to "win" a second election only through massive fraud.[9] Russia seemed poised to follow a similar trajectory. After all, Russia's economic reform had produced more hardship than that of any of those East European countries.[10] Moreover, Lech Wałęsa or Klaus did not initiate an unpopular civil war. Because communism came to Russia through revolution and not on the turrets of the Red Army, many analysts assumed that Communists enjoyed more legitimacy in Russia than in the rest of Eastern Europe.

How, then, did Boris Yeltsin win reelection in what most observers concluded was a relatively free and fair vote?[11] How can we explain the apparent defeat for reformist parties in December 1995 followed by a landslide victory for these same political forces only six months later? What does this electoral victory say about the structure of electoral politics in post-Soviet Russia generally?

Three interrelated factors combine to explain this outcome. First, the 1996 vote was not Russia's first direct election for a head of state but Russia's last "revolutionary" election in which voters were asked to choose between two fundamentally different systems. Understood as an election between several candidates with competing platforms and diverse personal strengths and weaknesses, Yeltsin's victory seems extraordinary. Understood as the last "referendum" on communism— a vote between two different political and economic systems—the outcome should have been expected. As in all elections from 1990 to 1996, the majority of Russians in this vote preferred the current system, or the prospects offered by the current system, to the Soviet ancien régime. Contrary to most Western analyses of Russian voter preferences, the balance between supporters and opponents of the new political and economic order has remained fairly stable in the first six years of Russian electoral history.

Second, what did change between December 1995 and June 1996 was the kind of election. The institutions governing this *presidential* vote shaped the electoral outcome differently from the previous two *parliamentary* elections in Russia. If Russia's mixed electoral system in 1993 and 1995 encouraged party proliferation and fragmentation, the 1996 presidential election provided incentives for polarization and consolidation. As in previous elections in Russia in the last decade, this polarized vote abetted the reformist cause. When given many choices, Russian voters in December 1993 and December 1995 dispersed their preferences among several parties and candidates. When given only two choices, in June 1991 (presidential election), April 1993 (referendum), December 1993 (constitutional referendum), and June and July 1996, the majority of Russians consistently opted for reform over regress. Predictions of Yeltsin's demise did not fully realize the importance of the role of institutions in shaping electoral outcomes.

Third, the campaign mattered. Yeltsin's team ran an effective, modern campaign that took into account the influences of these other two major variables. Gennadii Zyuganov, the communist challenger, did not. After flirting early in the campaign with a suboptimal strategy of acting like his opponents, Yeltsin realized that he could only win reelection by first establishing himself as the only leader capable of uniting all of Russia's reformist forces and then convincing Russian voters that he was the lesser of two evils. Ironically, Zyuganov's strategic objectives were similar to Yeltsin's—first become the focal point of Russia's opposition forces and then convince a majority of Russian voters that he was the lesser of two evils. His party's electoral victory in 1995 accomplished the first task even before the presidential campaign began. Zyuganov grossly miscalculated regarding the second objective, however, as his tilt toward nationalist and patriotic slogans served to reify his image as a radical, while not highlighting the destabilizing aspects of Yeltsin and his policies. Given the relatively predetermined effects of the first two variables, campaign strategy proved especially critical for determining the electoral outcome. A different campaign strategy by either Yeltsin or Zyuganov might have changed the results dramatically.

Taken together, these three sets of variables provide a sufficient explanation for why Yeltsin won. In highlighting these three sets of variables, however, this volume does not mean to suggest that other factors did not contribute to Yeltsin's victory. For instance, Yeltsin's virtual monopoly of the national media and his generous use of state largesse certainly contributed in some proportion to his electoral victory. As discussed below, however, these factors were not sufficient to produce a Yeltsin electoral victory. Instead, they are better understood as tactics or tools—a subset of factors under the general strategy of casting Yeltsin as the leader of reform and the lesser of two evils.

This study proceeds as follows. Chapter 1 focuses on voter attitudes, placing the Russian experience in a broad theoretical context regarding voting behavior. This chapter, which demonstrates why retrospective voting models provided an inappropriate framework for understanding this Russian election, underscores the importance of polarization and demonstrates its stability. This chapter also offers a theoretical explanation of the causes of Russian electoral polarization, highlighting how Russia's revolutionary transition to democracy and market capitalism has slowed the emergence of interest-based politics.

If voting preferences in Russia have been stable over the past six years, then why have election outcomes *looked* so different? Chapter 2 offers a partial explanation—institutions. Institutions, or the rules of the game structuring politics, in presidential elections have a different effect on the behavior of actors than the institutions that govern parliamentary elections. Chapter 2 explains, comparatively and within

Russia's own electoral history, how the rules of the game in the 1996 presidential election served to reinforce polarization within Russia's electorate, while rules structuring elections in 1993 and 1995 did not.

Chapters 3, 4, and 5 describe the electoral strategies pursued by Boris Yeltsin, Gennadii Zyuganov, and the other main contenders within the context of the set of electoral preferences and institutional constraints discussed in chapters 1 and 2. Although the strategies pursued by Boris Yeltsin and Gennadii Zyuganov constitute the focus of this section, other candidates and their strategies are discussed as they affected the two principal contenders.

Chapter 6 summarizes the results of the first round, describes electoral strategies between rounds, discusses the breakdown of the second-round results, and offers a brief summary of the main factors that influenced the outcome of the election, including a brief discussion of counterfactuals. Chapter 7 discusses possible scenarios in Russia's next presidential election, as well as the future of democratic consolidation in Russia more generally.

1

Revolutionary Transitions and Societal Polarization

The Role of Elections in Transitions

In most transitions to democracy, the successful completion of several electoral cycles helps consolidate the democratic system. First, electoral support for the "founding fathers" usually wanes. In first, or founding, elections, challengers of the old regime tend to score dramatic electoral victories. In second-round elections, the romantic era of transition usually ends as voter expectations—formed during transition—are almost never met.[1] This reaction against the new leaders has proven especially acute in transitions from communist rule because political transition has had to be accompanied by painful economic transformation.[2] Throughout Eastern Europe, most anticommunist leaders who won electoral victories in first elections lost to former communist leaders in second elections.[3]

This electoral reaction against political leaders who initiated economic reform is predicted by retrospective theories of voting behavior.[4] This approach to explaining elections posits that voter preferences are most directly influenced by individual "pocketbook" issues. As Ronald Reagan asked American voters in his presidential bid in 1980, "Are you better off or worse off today than you were four years ago?" Those who are better-off vote for incumbents, and those who are worse-off vote for challengers. In the postcommunist world, the majority is usually worse-off by the time of the second vote.

That the heroes of democratization during founding elections are voted out of office in the second round does not mark the end of democracy. On the contrary, the successful completion of a transfer of governmental power without a parallel change in regime constitutes a major milestone of democratic consolidation. In postcommunist countries in which Communists have come back to power, they have not attempted to restore the old political and economic order. In fact, these communist groups became social-democratic parties *before* coming to power, meaning that they took over government as supporters of the new regime.

A second consequence of the successful completion of several electoral cycles in democratic transitions is the consolidation of a party system. Founding elections tend to serve up the largest menu of choices to voters. Over time, however, these numbers dwindle as parties that do not win representation disappear. As O'Donnell and Schmitter concluded in their multicase study of transition from authoritarian rule:

> Founding elections seem to have a sort of freezing effect upon subsequent political developments. Where they are followed by successive iterations of the electoral process, few new parties get into the game, and many minor ones are likely to drop out.[5]

With time, voters also learn what their parties stand for, making them less likely to waste votes on fringe or nonviable parties.[6] Although declining in number, parties tend to increase in importance after a democratic transition as they emerge to play the central role intermediating interests between state and society. Every consolidated democracy in the world has a multiparty system.

Elections in Russia, however, have not yet produced either of these two results. Since 1989, Russians have voted a lot—four parliamentary elections (1989, 1990, 1993, and 1995), two presidential elections (1991 and 1996), four referenda (two in 1991, two in 1993), three rounds of elections for regional legislatures (1990, 1994, 1996), and two rounds of elections for regional heads of administration (the first in 1991 for republics [in 1993 for oblasts and *krays*] and the second in the fall of 1996).[7] Despite these significant numbers, elections have not produced a transfer of government power from the founding fathers to the Communists or some third force. Nor has a developed party system emerged. Why is Russia different? Why have elections in Russia not produced the same patterns and results that they have generated in other democratic transitions, and how did Russia's particular electoral history influence the presidential vote in 1996?

Russia's Revolutionary Transition in Comparative Context

For several years, Russia has been in transit from communist dictatorship to a pluralistic system. At one level, Russia's transition resembles transitions from authoritarian rule in other parts of the world.[8] At another level, however, the differences between Russia's transition and other nonrevolutionary transition are critical, both to explain the presidential elections in 1996 and to understand Russian politics more generally.[9]

First, all postcommunist transitions are distinguished from capitalist transitions by the scale of change. If transitions to democracies in capitalist countries involve primarily the transformation of the political system,[10] successful postcommunist transitions alter both the political and the socioeconomic system.[11] In the former communist world, this means moving from authoritarian to democratic rule while also creating a market system out of a command economy.[12] In doing so, successful postcommunist transformations destroy old classes, create new interest groups, and confuse, at least temporarily, most everyone else living through the transition.[13] Under these circumstances, interest cleavages are fashioned more by general attitudes about the revolutionary project than by particular economic, social, or even ethnic concerns. Conventional cleavages, which demarcate the contours of stable party systems, emerge only after consolidation of the new economic and political system.[14]

Such impediments to interest articulation and party formation are inherent to all postcommunist transitions.[15] Yet, unlike Russia, many countries in the former communist world already boast consolidated

multiparty systems, which suggests that the structure of societal interests alone cannot account for the prolonged polarization of Russian
politics.[16] A second feature of Russia's transition—the mode of transition—must be understood to explain Russia's prolonged period of
"revolutionary" politics.[17] Whereas successful transitions to democracy
generally (but not always) are facilitated by negotiated settlements,
interim constitutions, or pacts between the last rulers of the ancien
régime and the new leaders of the democratic polity, Russia's transition from communist rule was not negotiated or arrived at through
pacts.[18] Rather, forces for and against the ancien régime squared off
in a stalemate until one side won.[19] As a consequence of this kind of
transition, the losers (in 1991 and again in 1993) did not explicitly
accept the new rules of the game. Only in such a contested transition
could the deputy chairman of the Russian Communist Party declare
in 1996 that "the death of communism never happened . . . the Soviet
Union never collapsed, [and] people still think of themselves as Soviets."[20] The very boundaries of state, the organization of the political
system, and the kind of economic system remained contested issues,
prolonging polarized politics in Russia between those for the new
order and those against it.[21] Moreover, because Russia's revolutionary
transition has remained relatively peaceful, the leaders and resources
of the ancien régime have continued to play a much greater role in
shaping (and often impeding) the consolidation of new political and
economic institutions. Advocates of restoration remained players in
Russian politics well after they had lost their political power.

The numerous labels assigned to these two camps have produced
confusion and misinterpretation of Russian electoral outcomes both
in Russia and, especially, in the West. In part, this confusion stems
from the fact that those once defending the ancien régime became
challengers to the new status quo after 1991 and vice versa. In other
words, the Communists were the "conservatives" before 1991, seeking
to preserve the established order, whereas anticommunist leaders and
groups—called in Russia "the democrats"—constituted the "liberals"
or "progressives" seeking to change the old order. By 1993, these terms
had become even more confused as the "democrats" now in power
were seeking to preserve the new order, whereas the Communists had
become the opposition seeking to alter the status quo.

Observers get bogged down in defining "reform," assuming that greater precision in characterizing Yeltsin's policies will produce a better explanation of electoral outcomes. Those in search of political party formation also (mis)apply categories such as *left* and *right* or labels such as *liberal, social democrat,* and *conservative* to a political landscape in which these terms have lost their meaning. However confusing to outsiders, the basic contours of the bipolar ideological divide seem to be understood by Russian voters as follows.

Labels for Russia's Bipolar Political Society

Zyuganov	*Yeltsin*
Against the status quo	For the status quo
Opposition	Pro-Yeltsin
Left	Right
Right	Left
Antireform	Proreform
Communist	Anticommunist
Conservative	Liberal
Nationalist	Democrat

Although opinion polls have demonstrated that centrist and nationalist labels produce confusion in the electorate, the basic divide between these two camps is easily recognized.[22]

This interpretation of Russian politics provides a different theoretical framework for understanding and explaining Russia's 1996 electoral outcome than that offered by conventional electoral or transition models. In highlighting the high degree of elite and societal polarization, this approach suggests that Russian voter preferences are best understood as falling within two broad categories: those in support of the current course and those against it. Survey data about voter attitudes may provide a more complex picture about preferences regarding specific issues, but the framework outlined in this study suggests that attitudes about the system, not positions on specific issues, motivated voters in this election. When confronted with choices between candidates representing alternative political and socioeconomic systems, voter are less likely to make decisions based strictly on personal, egocentric preferences.[23] Rather, during periods of revolutionary change, when national politics directly affect individual lives, we should expect voter concerns about systemic issues to be more salient than "pocketbook" issues.

Relatedly, this framework for understanding Russian politics suggests that Russian voters should be more inclined to make choices based on expectations about the future rather than mere short-term calculations about past events, economic or otherwise.[24] During static periods, several studies of U.S. voting behavior have demonstrated that voters make electoral decisions based on past outcomes rather than future policies.[25] At the same time, advocates of the retrospective voting hypothesis have recognized conditions in which such behavior is less likely. As Morris Fiorina writes:

> Traditional retrospective voting should be most evident on issues that are not bound up in strongly held ideologies and/or among citizens who do not conceptualize political affairs in ideological terms. Conversely, I doubt that the traditional theory of retrospective voting will shed much light on the behavior of the highly ideological or the disposition of issues considered touchstones of particular ideologies.[26]

Russia's presidential election in 1996 constituted one of these rare, highly ideological elections identified by Fiorina. Under these conditions, then, we expect Russian voters to have been less concerned with evaluating the incumbent's past performance and more interested in choosing the candidate that most closely represented their conception of Russia's future economic and political system. The assumption of prospective voting does not mean that the past is unimportant, as voters do not make prospective calculations in a historical void. On the contrary, a voter's best information about the future is based on past experiences. In the Russian case, most voters (except the youngest) had lived in both systems—the system represented by the communist candidate, Gennadii Zyuganov, and that represented by Boris Yeltsin. In making calculations about the expected utility of these systems in the future, therefore, they were able to compare systems and did not have to rely solely on promises about future policies.

Once the revolutionary transition is complete, then, we should expect retrospective voting to dominate, as the trend in Eastern Europe demonstrates. The model of protracted transition sketched above implies that Russia's 1996 presidential vote should not be understood as the second election "after" transition (in which we should observe retrospective voting and consequently opposition victory) but the last election "of" the transition.

These claims about prospective voting based on calculations about macroissues rather than primitive individual utility also implicitly refute pork barrel explanations, business-cycle theories, and media manipulation as important determinants of the electoral outcome.[27] If voters are motivated first and foremost by assessments of competing "systems," they should not be influenced by short-term economic changes, positive or negative.[28] From the logic outlined here, attempts by Yeltsin to manipulate economic trends in the short run or to allocate new government transfers to targeted voters could have had only a marginal impact on the electoral outcome. When voters are choosing between "communism" and "capitalism," they cannot be bought off by promises of marginal, short-term individual gains. More generally, candidate promises about the future that do not correspond to past behavior rarely influence voter decisions.[29] Again, in the Russian presidential election, voters had hard information about the past performance of both candidates from which they could form realistic expectations about future behavior. This argument also assumes that media images or television propaganda that ran counter to historically formed conceptions of candidates and their positions had only a marginal influence.[30]

This argument about Russia's revolutionary transition also suggests why party identification should not be an important determinant of voter behavior. Parties could not play a determinative role in this election because an articulate party system did not exist in Russia at the time.[31] The crystallized divide between those for and against the "revolution" has impeded interest-based party development and the emergence of third candidates. When politics are polarized, ideological differences, class divisions, or ethnic identities or all three are subsumed by two broad categories—reform or antireform, status quo or status quo ante.

EVIDENCE OF STABLE POLARIZATION

When guided by this assumption about revolutionary polarization, the electoral results of elections over the past six years look relatively stable, both in the aggregate and when broken down regionally. In the aggregate, all of Russia's referenda and presidential votes—that is, votes that structurally tend to divide the electorate into two camps—have yielded the same basic results (see table 1).[32] Although guided by a different logic, explained in the next chapter, even Russia's parliamentary votes in 1993 and 1995 reflect this stability in numbers between those for and against the status quo (see table 2).

The sum of the reformist vote in these parliamentary elections appears lower than the anticommunist vote in the referenda and presidential votes because the multiple choices offered in parliamentary elections allowed voters to support not only "reform" or "opposition" parties but also so-called centrist parties as well as special-interest electoral blocs. Although difficult to measure on the individual level, the participation of these centrist and special-interest groups appears to have diluted the reformist vote on the aggregate level.[33]

Geographic and demographic voting patterns from previous Russian elections clearly delineate the contours of this polarization within Russia's electorate. First, geographically, the urban-rural divide demarcates the main line of division between those supporting the status quo and those who do not.[34] People living in big cities (populations greater than one million) have tended to support anticommunist candidates, whereas people in rural areas have tended to support communist candidates.[35] Age has been a second cleavage dividing supporters and opponents of change. Russia's oldest voters have been most resistant to Yeltsin's reforms, whereas Russia's youngest voters have enthusiastically supported reform.[36] Third, and not surprisingly, supporters of reform have tended to be much richer than opponents

Table 1   Two Camps of the Russian Electorate

	Reform Vote (Yeltsin) (in %)	Opposition Vote (in %)
June 1991	58.6	36.0
April 1993	58.7	39.3
December 1993	58.4*	41.6*
July 1996	53.8	40.3

* This is the breakdown of the vote for the constitution, not the parliamentary elections.

Table 2   Russian Parliamentary Votes, 1993 and 1995

	Core Reformist (in %)	Core Opposition (in %)
1993	27.5	43.3
1995	25.5	42.5

of reform.[37] These factors distinguishing the battle lines between the forces for and against reform should not necessarily be considered independent variables: Russia's poorest people live in the countryside in the southern part of the country, whereas Russia's richest live in northern urban areas. What is striking is that Russia's two electoral camps have been clearly defined and stable throughout Russia's electoral history.

2

Presidential versus Parliamentary Elections

For many analysts, the alleged dissipation of polarized politics in the 1993 and 1995 parliamentary elections compelled them to suggest that the next election—the presidential election—would also be shaped by multiparty politics. Such analyses, however, failed to account for how institutions shape choices and subsequent outcomes. In particular, Russia's presidential electoral law structured the 1996 vote differently than the rules that guided parliamentary elections in 1995 or 1993. Most important, Russia's parliamentary elections stimulated fragmentation and protoparty development, whereas the presidential election reinforced the polarizing tendencies in society identified above.[1]

Although half of Russia's parliamentary seats were allocated in single-mandate districts, the other half were determined by a national system of proportional representation (PR) in 1993 and again in 1995.[2] As in other countries, Russia's PR system encouraged the proliferation of political parties and provided few incentives for party consolidation.[3] In 1993, thirteen parties participated in the Duma elections; in 1995, forty-three parties made the ballot.

In contrast, presidential elections tend to produce two-party systems, majoritarianism, and polarization.[4] This is because the electoral district magnitude for electing a president is usually one—that is, the entire country chooses one person for president.[5] Elections in which only one candidate can win create strong incentives to consolidate alliances and narrow the field before the vote, pushing political systems toward bipolarity and majoritarianism.[6] Because the winner takes all for a fixed term, presidential elections become more important and confrontational than other kinds of elections. As Juan Linz notes, "The zero-sum game raises the stakes in a presidential election for winners and losers, and inevitably increases the tension and the polarization."[7] The combination of the extreme ideological divide between Yeltsin and Zyuganov and Russia's superpresidential system, which grants extraordinary powers of the president, magnified the stakes of this presidential election even more.

Within the universe of presidential systems, some electoral laws are more narrowing than others.[8] Plurality systems in which the winner is the candidate with the most votes after one round of voting generate the strongest incentives for two-party systems. Electoral laws that include a runoff between the top two candidates in the first round tend to be more fragmentary, as they offer incentives for candidates to stay in the race. For instance, in elections with a runoff, underdog candidates can hope to squeeze into the second round and then unite all the forces that lost in the first round to produce a winning coalition in the second. Between rounds, defeated candidates from the first round can attempt to trade their endorsement of one of top two finishers in exchange for individual, ideological, or organizational gain.

Russia's presidential electoral law requires a runoff if no one receives more than 50 percent of the votes in the first round. Consequently, consolidation into large blocs did not take place before the first round, and eleven candidates qualified for the first ballot. Because no one expected any candidate to win more than 50 percent in the first round, this two-ballot system encouraged third-party or "spoiler" candidates to remain in the race until the end.[9] This electoral system even raised the specter of surprise outcomes, whereby a newcomer such as General Aleksandr Lebed might sneak past Yeltsin in the first round and then defeat Zyuganov in a runoff.[10] For the two frontrunners, the two-ballot system required careful campaign strategy between rounds. Nonetheless, the more general polarizing effects of a presidential race, as opposed to a parliamentary party-list election, shaped the contours of this election from the beginning. As discussed below, polarization and bifurcation also influenced the initial campaign strategy of all the major candidates.[11]

The electoral cycle constitutes a second institutional factor that shapes electoral outcomes.[12] When parliamentary and presidential elections occur concurrently, they can influence each other. The converse is equally true: That Russia's presidential and parliamentary elections did not take place at the same time helps explain why the outcomes varied so widely. In June 1991, during the referenda of April 1993 and December 1993, and again in the 1996 presidential vote, Yeltsin's participation and the binary nature of these votes helped polarize the Russian electorate into two camps. When divided in such a way, majorities have coalesced consistently for Yeltsin and his policies. Conversely, in the 1993 and 1995 parliamentary elections, when Yeltsin did not participate and the choices on the ballot were greater than two, the outcome was less positive for liberal parties and candidates.[13]

In both these parliamentary elections, Yeltsin had institutional and political incentives to encourage fragmentation among his party supporters because these divisions (1) weakened the Duma's effectiveness, (2) impeded the development of strong liberal political parties that could counter or constrain Yeltsin's own personal power, (3) discredited potential presidential candidates, including Viktor Chernomyrdin and Grigorii Yavlinsky, and (4) helped fuel support for Yeltsin as the only person capable of uniting reformist forces and defeating the Communists.[14] Yeltsin's team deemed fragmentation within Russia's reformist forces in the December 1995 elections especially important to Yeltsin's electoral prospects the following year.[15] If Chernomyrdin, Yavlinsky, or Lebed had emerged from the December 1995 elections as a viable competitor with a chance to defeat Zyuganov, reformist forces and voters quickly would have gravitated to one of them, not Yeltsin. (In 1995, remember, Yeltsin polled even with or sometimes behind these potential challengers from the reformist or anticommunist side of Russia's political ledger.)

Beyond these general institutional effects, other regulations outlined in the presidential electoral law had only a marginal impact on the outcome of the election. As in previous Russian elections, the threshold for registering as a presidential candidate—one million signatures—did not constitute a major obstacle as signatures could be bought easily. In fact, two unknown but wealthy entrepreneurs—Martin Shakkum and Vladimir Brynstalov—managed to collect or buy or both one million signatures even though they both barely won that many votes in the actual election.[16]

The law on presidential elections established strict limits on campaign spending but was not enforced. Estimates of spending by the Yeltsin campaign ranged from $100 to $500 million, way above the limit of roughly $3 million.[17]

Recapping the Contextual Factors

Well before the 1996 campaign began, then, the general structure of Russia's electorate and the rules of the game that governed presidential votes defined the parameters conditioning and constraining Russia's presidential campaign. In a repetition of Russian elections in 1995 and over the last several years more generally, the presidential race started in the context of a polarized and bifurcated electorate—those for the status quo and those against it.[18] Although Russian society was becoming more differentiated and complex as the market began to take hold, the 1996 election still (and probably for the last time) divided society into those seeking continuity with the present course of reform and those seeking change. This polarization was reinforced by the fact that this was a presidential vote, not a parliamentary election.

Following from this polarized electorate, only two kinds of candidates could be competitive—those supporting the current system and those opposing it. Given the logic of polarized electoral politics in Russia, potential "third-way" candidates had no serious chance.[19] Accordingly, issues of the campaign had to fit along one cleavage line; third positions or nuanced stances did not resonate.

When understood through the prism of bipolar, revolutionary politics, the initial balance of support between Russia's two camps looked rather stable. Contrary to most immediate analyses of the 1995 election, Russian voters had not become more leftist or more nationalist in the past few years. As indicated in December 1995, core support for the opposition was substantial, at almost 40 percent, but still well below a majority. At the same time, core support for a reformist was a minority of the electorate but still significant.

Even before the campaign began, then, Russia's polarized electorate and the structure of presidential votes left two central questions unanswered. First, these two variables suggested that a status quo candidate and an opposition candidate would face each other in the final round but did not specify who those candidates would be. The Communist Party's parliamentary victory in December 1995 clearly established Gennadii Zyuganov as the leader of the opposition, but in January 1996 no one candidate looked like the obvious front-runner on the other side of the ledger. Second, core support for both reform and antireform was less than 50 percent, meaning that both communist and anticommunist candidates had to reach beyond their traditional electoral bases to win the second round. The amorphous "center"—that part of the Russian electorate that did not consolidate behind a single party in 1995—ultimately would decide the winner of the 1996 presidential election. The campaign strategies adopted by Yeltsin and Zyuganov—first to establish themselves as the front-runners of the reform and opposition camps and then to reach this median voter—constitute the third and critical set of factors that shaped the final electoral outcome.

3

The Yeltsin Campaign

The Aborted Soskovets Strategy

In the three years leading up to the opening of the presidential campaign in 1996, Yeltsin and his government had adopted an increasingly nationalist and authoritarian orientation. The surprising results of the December 1993 parliamentary elections helped stimulate this new profile. In this election, Russia's Choice, the proreform and pro-Yeltsin electoral bloc, fared miserably. Although expected to win as much as 40 percent of the popular vote, Russia's Choice garnered only 15.5 percent.[1] At the same time, Vladimir Zhirinovsky's Liberal Democratic Party captured almost 25 percent of the popular vote. Although shocking, Zhirinovsky's protofascist views, law-and-order rhetoric, and racist undertones resonated with an electorate tired of both the communist past and the "democratic" present.

These election results apparently demonstrated to Yeltsin's inner circle of advisers the need to change Yeltsin's image, rhetoric, and allies.[2] If Yeltsin was going to win reelection in June 1996, he had to act and talk more like Zhirinovsky and less like the "democrats." The goal was not for Yeltsin to mimic Zhirinovsky but rather to position the incumbent as a candidate between Zhirinovsky and the reformers or, better yet, as a candidate who personified both political platforms.[3] Soon thereafter, Yeltsin presented his first State of the Federation speech (*Poslanie Prezidenta*) in which he called for strengthening the state, highlighting first and foremost his plans to crack down on crime. Yeltsin also got tough, at least rhetorically, with his opponents, be they Latvians, the North Atlantic Treaty Organization, or Most Bank.[4] Bombing Chechnya was the most dramatic but by no means the first demonstration of Yeltsin's new nationalistic and aggressive look.

A second consequence of the December 1993 elections, and a contributing factor to Yeltsin's new political orientation, was a deepening division between Yeltsin and his immediate circle of advisers on the one hand and the reformist political leaders and organizations on the other. Because their historical origins were different, the alliance between Yeltsin and the democrats had always been unstable.[5] Yeltsin rose to power as a populist, anticorruption, anti-Moscow Communist Party boss from the Urals. Eventually, his maverick style clashed with the staid practices of the Communist Party elite in Moscow, forcing him to look beyond the Soviet establishment for political allies after his ouster as a candidate member of the Politburo in 1987. He eventually found new comrades among the liberal, Western-oriented democratic movements, which by 1990 had mobilized into a united front called Democratic Russia based primarily in Moscow, Saint Petersburg, and the Urals. This powerful alliance swept Yeltsin into power in June 1991, resisted the August 1991 coup attempt, and then formed Russia's first noncommunist government.

This alliance, however, never fused into one political organization. Yeltsin never joined Democratic Russia but instead stayed "above" party politics.[6] Moreover, tension between Yeltsin's aides from Sverdlovsk and the team of young economists around Yegor Gaidar continued throughout Gaidar's tenure as first deputy prime minister and then prime minister.[7] By the time of the December 1993 parliamentary elections, Yeltsin refused to endorse Gaidar's Russia's Choice even though several of his cabinet ministers were members. After the election, the gap between these two camps widened even further. Gaidar and Boris Fyodorov, the liberal finance minister, resigned from Yeltsin's government, leaving just one member of Gaidar's original team— Anatolii Chubais—within shouting distance of the president. Over the course of 1994, the president and his Kremlin advisers became even more isolated from both reformist political organizations as well as the government and its leader, Prime Minister Chernomyrdin.[8] During this period, the so-called party of war, led by First Deputy Prime Minister Oleg Soskovets and presidential "bodyguard" Aleksandr Korzhakov, played an increasingly important role in defining presidential policy.[9]

The results of the 1995 parliamentary elections served to reinforce, at least initially, the power of these hard-liners in the Kremlin. In their analysis, the 1995 vote demonstrated that the democrats were a spent political force. Russia's leading reformist party, Grigorii Yavlinsky's Yabloko, won only 6.9 percent of the popular vote, while the next largest reformist party, Yegor Gaidar's Democratic Choice of Russia, won an abysmal 3.9 percent. Even the prime minister's more centrist bloc, Our Home Is Russia, garnered only 10 percent. In the opinion of Yeltsin's hard-line advisers, campaigning for president as a democrat would be a recipe for failure. Soskovets, Korzhakov, and their allies also evaluated the strong showing of ultranationalist Vladimir Zhirinovsky as a sign that Russian voters yearned for a strong, decisive leader in the Kremlin who would fight crime, terrorism, and disorder.[10] To win in June 1996, therefore, Yeltsin would have to adopt similar positions. Finally, this camp within the Kremlin interpreted the communist victory in the 1995 parliamentary elections as a protest vote against the current economic reform program. To win in 1996, therefore, Yeltsin was advised to radically alter his reform program and reform team.

Guided initially by these assessments about Russian electoral preferences, Yeltsin launched his new campaign strategy in January.[11] In an apparent final break with the democrats, Yeltsin fired three key reformers in his government—Foreign Minister Andrei Kozyrev, Chief of Staff Sergei Filatov, and First Deputy Prime Minister Anatolii Chubais. In replacing Chubais with Vladimir Kadannikov, the director of Russia's largest automobile factory, Yeltsin wanted to signal an end of radical economic reform and the beginning of an economic policy more friendly to enterprise directors and workers.[12] Soon after removing Chubais, Yeltsin ordered the immediate payment of back wages to government workers, totaling more than $700 million dollars. The following month, Yeltsin delivered a critical annual report (*Poslanie*) to the Federal Assembly in which he lambasted his government for not increasing social spending, for failing to compensate people's savings from the 1992 price liberalization, and for neglecting agricultural and military reform. He also ordered greater protection of Russian enterprises, a declaration that was followed up by an announcement of a series of new measures to raise import tariffs. Although vowing to continue market reforms, Yeltsin's speech sounded more like an opposition statement than an address from a sitting president. As CPRF leader Gennadii Zyuganov remarked, "At least a third of the speech has been copied from Communist Party documents."[13]

Yeltsin replaced Kozyrev with Evgenii Primakov, a survivor from the Soviet era whose appointment both Zhirinovsky and the Communists praised. Yeltsin's new chief of staff, Nikolai Yegorov, was considered a hard-line nationalist who spearheaded the original invasion of Chechnya in 1994.[14] These two new appointments were designed to give Yeltsin's team a tougher, more nationalistic look. Yeltsin then matched words with deeds, ordering a massive use of force against Chechen fighters and their hostages in Pervomaiskoe, Dagestan, in January. The assault proved disastrous, killing many civilians while allowing the Chechen leaders to escape. Humiliated once again by the Chechen rebels, Yeltsin vowed to end the war through military victory, not negotiation.

Given this "new look" strategy, Yeltsin not surprisingly appointed Oleg Soskovets to head up his reelection campaign team. At the same time, Nikolai Yegorev, his new chief of staff, and Korzhakov also assumed major responsibilities in the campaign effort.

Although perhaps skilled at Kremlin court politics, Soskovets proved inept at electoral politics.[15] Having never participated in public politics, let alone a presidential campaign in the largest country in the world, Soskovets failed in his first major task of the campaign—the signature drive to register Boris Yeltsin as a candidate.[16] Instead of organizing public groups and social organizations to collect signatures, Soskovets relied exclusively on government bureaucrats. This proved to be a terrible mistake. Yeltsin wanted to be registered by February 15, but a week before this self-imposed deadline, the reelection campaign was well short of the million signatures needed.[17]

Already by the end of January, opponents of Soskovets and company had begun to argue before Yeltsin that this "new look" strategy was bound to fail.[18] Soon after the parliamentary elections in December 1995, Georgii Satarov, Yeltsin's adviser on political affairs, assembled a "brainstorming" group to write the president's annual address and plot campaign strategy. This team, which met at a group of dachas in Valinskoe just outside Moscow, quickly concluded that Yeltsin could only win as the candidate of reform and stability.[19] If he tried to compete for the nationalist and communist vote, he would lose.

Satarov's group quickly won allies among Russia's business community, who had the most to lose from a communist electoral victory. Assembled in Davos, Switzerland, for the annual meeting of the World Economic Forum, several key Russian businessmen agreed that something drastic had to be done to rescue Yeltsin's campaign.[20] Significantly, archrivals Vladimir Gusinskii from Most and Boris Berezovskii of Logovaz decided to bury their differences for the duration of the campaign and work together to reelect Boris Yeltsin.[21] Because Gusinskii owned NTV television (channel four) and Berezovskii was the chairman of the Board of ORT (channel one), this strategic alliance was critical.

Yeltsin, however, had to be convinced. In late January, Anatolii Chubais stretched a meeting planned for twenty minutes into two and a half hours in an attempt to convince Yeltsin to switch teams. Until this meeting, Yeltsin evidently had no idea that he was twenty points behind Gennadii Zyuganov in the polls. Soon thereafter, Berezovskii and his business colleagues met with the president and pledged to finance his campaign only if he hired a new campaign team. Within the Kremlin, Viktor Ilyushin became the main advocate for a change in the campaign team and campaign strategy. Decisive advice also came from Yeltsin's daughter, Tatyana Dyachenko, who eventually helped to convince her father of the need to remove Soskovets.[22]

The Ilyushin/Chubais Team

By February, Anatolii Chubais had organized a small group of analysts who began to plot an alternative campaign strategy for Yeltsin. Satarov's team also continued its work, focusing on the president's campaign platform, while Sergei Filatov began preparations for a third nongovernmental organization that was to serve as the united front of parties and social groups behind the president. In March, Yeltsin finally invited the shadow campaign structures to assume primary responsibility for his reelection effort. The official structure of the campaign, however, remained confused and decentralized.

Formally, Yeltsin himself replaced Soskovets as the head of the campaign on March 23. At the same time, Yeltsin appointed a new campaign "council" that included people from both the old and the new campaign teams, including old figures such as Aleksandr Korzhakov, Nikolai Yegorov, and Mikhail Barsukov, the head of the FSB (the former KGB), as well as new people such as Prime Minister Viktor Chernomyrdin, Viktor Ilyushin, Moscow mayor Yurii Luzhkov, Deputy Prime Ministers Yurii Yarov and Sergei Shakhrai, NTV television general director Igor Malashenko, and Yeltsin's daughter, Tatyana Dyachenko.[23] In effect, this council subsumed the original campaign structure as a way to neutralize the Soskovets/Korzhakov team.[24] Underneath this new council, new parallel campaign structures emerged that eventually assumed full responsibility for the execution of the campaign.

At the strategic level, two competing organizations formed. The team originally assembled by Soskovets—Korzhakov, Barsukov, Yegorov—continued to be part of the campaign. This team was located on the ninth floor of the Presidential Hotel, the eventual headquarters of all of Yeltsin's campaigns. Organizationally, this team had several nationwide structures at its disposal, including the FSB, the Federal Agency for Government Communications and Information (FAPSI), regional representatives of Korzhakov's analytic center, as well as several heads of administration who Korzhakov helped appoint. Aside from intelligence gathering and monitoring campaign spending, however, these structures played only a marginal role. According to Chubais, other parts of the campaign were not privy to the intelligence gathering done by Korzhakov.[25]

Chubais chaired the other main strategy group. Because he had served as the main liaison between the Yeltsin campaign and Russia's business community, he used the power of the purse to organize central aspects of the campaign around himself and his team. Within Chubais's team, Igor Malashenko assumed the critical assignment of television advertising and enhancing the president's image.[26] Duplicating Yegorov's work under Soskovets, Sergei Shakhrai took primary responsibility for working with regional leaders. Aleksandr Olson and his company, the Foundation for Public Opinion, were hired to provide polling data and research for the campaign. Satarov's group, now overlapping with Chubais's team, wrote the campaign platform and provided position papers, speech writing (principally by Aleksandr Urmanov), and analysis to the Chubais team. Dyachenko served as the direct line to the candidate.[27]

Nationwide, the campaign consisted of two parallel structures. Yurii Yarov, a deputy prime minister in Chernomyrdin's government, took primary responsibility for official organizational work. Under Yarov, the Yeltsin campaign employed representatives throughout Russia who usually served in the local administration. In addition to this official structure, several leaders and organizations claimed to be Boris Yeltsin's nongovernmental sponsors. Earlier in the year, Vladimir Shumeiko asserted that his new social organization/quasi party—Reform's New Course—would spearhead Yeltsin's reelection drive. At the same time, leaders of Our Home Is Russia claimed to be Yeltsin's primary campaign organization. After weeks of positioning and infighting, however, Sergei Filatov eventually founded the central nationwide campaign structure called the All-Russian Movement for Social Support for the President, or ODOP in Russian. ODOP served as an umbrella for more than 250 parties, unions, civic groups, and social organizations supporting Yeltsin's candidacy. The twenty-one organizations that founded ODOP included such diverse groups as Our Home Is Russia, Aleksandr Yakovlev's Social Democratic Party, Lev Ponomarev's Democratic Russia, Vladimir Shumeiko's New Course, and Arkadii Volskii's Union of Industrialists and Entrepreneurs.[28] At its founding congress on April 6, 1996, ODOP established itself as the most visible and organized movement supporting Boris Yeltsin.

Filatov located ODOP's headquarters in the Presidential Hotel, one floor above Korzhakov's deputies. Once established, ODOP and Chubais's group formed the core of the Yeltsin reelection drive. This team hired Russia's leading campaign advisers, image-making consultants, and advertising agencies to work on the campaign. Malashenko hired Video International, the agency that supplies NTV with most of its advertising and television programs, to produce Yeltsin's television spots, posters, and leaflets. Direct mail and additional poster contracts went to Mikhail Semenov, the director of Russia's largest direct mail firm. Igor Mintusev and Yekaterina Yegerova of the campaign consulting firm Nikola M were hired to work on Yeltsin's image. The Yeltsin campaign employed several media consultants to place favorable articles in the national and regional press.[29] Filatov's staff also hired dozens of campaign managers from several different political parties. By the end of the campaign, virtually every major research firm, think tank, and public relations company had received some work from the wealthy Yeltsin campaign.

In addition to these efforts sponsored directly by the Yeltsin team, several companies "volunteered" support to the president. For instance, *Kommersant'*, one of Russia's leading business newspapers, published a special anticommunist newspaper called *Ne Dai Bog* (God forbid). At ORT television, a special committee in charge of programming orchestrated a steady stream of anticommunist films and documentaries that aired on the station before the election. Perhaps most significantly, Vladimir Lisovskii organized the Vote or Lose campaign, a $10 million series of MTV-like television programs and rock concerts aimed at mobilizing the youth vote.[30]

Outside Moscow, the Yeltsin campaign maintained its organizational confusion, with four independent entities claiming to represent the campaign. In every region, the official campaign (under Yarov) appointed its own representative. In parallel, both ODOP and Our Home Is Russia (though a member of ODOP) also fielded their own representatives and offices. A fourth amorphous network called Narodnyi Dom (National house) was established throughout the country. Officially, this organization provided nongovernmental consultative social services to citizens and served as a kind of social club to local residents, complete with free coffee and occasional entertainment. Unofficially, campaign money was transferred through this network to avoid official detection.

Relations among these organizations varied from region to region. In some places, the regional offices of the campaign, ODOP, Our Home Is Russia, and Narodnyi Dom acted as one; in others they refused to interact at all. As a whole, however, this set of different organizations offered the national campaign tremendous flexibility. For instance, in regions with strong local parties and civic groups, ODOP assumed primary responsibility for campaign activities. In regions with weaker nongovernmental organizations, however, Moscow could channel primary support to the official campaign representative and avoid being captive to the marginal local political groups. In doing so, Yeltsin's team managed to forge an unlikely alliance, however temporary, between the "party of power" and the "democrats."

Stage One: Polarization

Once the liberals assumed control of Yeltsin's reelection effort, the overall strategy of the campaign became more clearly defined. Although Yeltsin's State of the Union address might have co-opted many phrases from the CPRF's program,[31] the new campaign team did not believe that Yeltsin could win by acting like the Communists or the Nationalists. Nor did they think that Yeltsin could win on his own record. After all, Yeltsin's record over the past five years included a prolonged and painful economic reform, a tragic and avoidable mini–civil war in downtown Moscow in October 1993, and a full-fledged war in Chechnya for the past two years. To win, Yeltsin and his campaign had to make this vote yet another referendum on communism. Voters had to understand (or be made to believe) that they were choosing between two systems, not two candidates.

To succeed in polarizing the election into two antithetical camps, several steps had to be accomplished. First, Yeltsin had to again be made palatable and believable as a candidate of reform. According to Igor Bunin, the director of the Center for Political Technologies and a key adviser to the Yeltsin campaign, focus groups conducted in January indicated that Yeltsin's negatives were higher than any other candidate's.[32] When asked to list Yeltsin's principal attributes, "drunk," "ill," and "out of touch with the common person" made the top five. "Experienced" was the only moderately positive adjective to make the list. In response, Yeltsin and his advisers worked actively to alter this image. Most dramatically, Yeltsin lost more than twenty pounds and stopped drinking. To underscore his new vigor, Yeltsin began to appear frequently in active settings, including tours of mine shafts and dances with rock stars. To address his drinking problem, Yeltsin tried to portray himself as a "typical" Russian; when asked if he abused alcohol, he replied:

> To say yes would be untrue. To say no would not be convincing. Here people will not believe it unless they chcck it themselves. They would even say: "What kind of Russian man are you if you can't drink?" So I will only say that I can drink, but that I don't abuse alcohol![33]

To rectify his image as a person out of touch with the problems of the average person, Yeltsin visited two dozen cities in four months.[34] At all these stops, Yeltsin's campaign ensured that the candidate met with common voters and that national television crews were there.

More generally, campaign officials hoped to recast Yeltsin as a leader of strong power (*silnaya vlast'*), a forceful, decisive figure who could lead Russian through troubled times.[35] This strong image was accompanied by messages about Yeltsin as a father figure both for his own family and for the nation.[36] To develop this theme, the Yeltsin campaign (primarily on television) emphasized the importance of family issues. These messages were then followed up with images of Yeltsin as a father.

Proving that Yeltsin was healthy, powerful, and fatherly, however, was not enough. Yeltsin also had to address several negative policies associated with his presidency. Public opinion polls identified two negative issues that towered above the rest: unpaid wages and pensions and the war in Chechnya.[37]

Repaying back wages thus became one of Yeltsin's first campaign promises. On numerous occasions, Kremlin officials had blamed the wage payments crisis for the CPRF's strong showing in the December 1995 parliamentary elections.[38] To demonstrate resolve, Yeltsin fired First Deputy Prime Minister Anatolii Chubais in January, blaming him for the crisis. The following month, Yeltsin sacked the governors of Saratov and Arkhangelsk oblasts for allegedly misusing federal funds and holding federal funds that had been transferred to pay wages. In May, the presidential administration removed four more governors (from Vologda, Bryansk, and Amur oblasts and Stavropol Krai) for the same reasons; someone besides the president had to be blamed for the wage payment crisis.[39] To dramatize the issue, Yeltsin received daily reports from his adviser for economy policy, Aleksandr Livshits.[40] Television and print covered the issue daily until April 1, 1996, when Livshits announced that all back wages had been paid.[41]

Ending the war in Chechnya was seen as even more central, however, to winning back electoral support from traditional reformist voters.[42] Thus on April 2, 1996, in a dramatic speech covered by all three national networks, Yeltsin announced that he was ordering the withdrawal of Russian troops from Chechnya and beginning negotiations to end the war. Soon thereafter, Yeltsin signed a peace treaty with Chechen resistance leader Zelimkhan Yandarbiev in the Kremlin. The next day Yeltsin made a dramatic, albeit brief, visit to Chechnya to symbolize the importance of the peace treaty.[43] Fighting, of course, continued after the peace accord was signed, but because Yeltsin enjoyed a virtual monopoly over the national media, he could maintain the myth that the war was ending.

The conclusion of the Chechen war (or the created appearance of same) fulfilled the major precondition for many of Russia's reformers to unify behind Yeltsin. Lev Ponomarev and Father Gleb Yakunin, human rights activists and the founders of Democratic Russia, announced their support for Yeltsin, stating that it was better to reelect a "liberal" Communist than a conservative Communist. Yegor Gaidar and his Democratic Choice of Russia (DVR) also agreed to endorse Yeltsin after the Chechen peace.[44] Although the DVR's endorsement alone was unlikely to deliver many votes to Yeltsin, the move did allow hundreds of DVR activists to join the campaign.[45] In dozens of regions, DVR organizers assumed major roles. Most important, the very act of major political leaders lining up behind Boris Yeltsin created the impression that the "democrats" were reuniting for the first time since 1991. Even a few Yabloko regional organizations broke ranks with their presidential candidate and endorsed Yeltsin.

Yavlinsky and other members of the so-called third force, however, posed a true threat to the polarization strategy. Marginalizing these alternative candidates, therefore, became an early focus of the Yeltsin campaign. Progress with Aleksandr Lebed came first. Even before the campaign season began, several different Yeltsin allies had approached the retired general to discuss possible forms of cooperation. With no financial or organizational resources and little campaign experience, Lebed had struggled even to register as a candidate.[46] Yeltsin, first through his emissary Aleksandr Korzhakov in March and later in May in person, offered Lebed a deal.[47] In return for an endorsement after the first round, Yeltsin and his campaign would allow Lebed to work with financial backers and campaign consultants close to the president and then would offer him a major post in Yeltsin's government after the first round.[48] For Yeltsin, the pact was a brilliant move. By staying in the race to the end, Lebed would attract voters that would never have voted for Yeltsin in the first round.[49] With Lebed in the Kremlin after the first round, these voters might then cast their support behind the Yeltsin-Lebed ticket. The deal also meant that Lebed would not cooperate with Yavlinsky. For Lebed, the deal was also too attractive to refuse, as it gave him the opportunity to compete actively in the first round of the campaign, assured him of a post-election political career, and thereby propelled him to the front of the pack of potential successors to Yeltsin. The candidates began to cooperate effectively in April and closed the deal in May.[50]

Once the deal with Lebed was secure, negotiations with Yavlinsky assumed much less importance. Without Lebed, Yavlinsky posed no serious threat to Yeltsin in the first round. Unlike Lebed's supporters, Yeltsin campaign managers expected Yavlinsky backers to support Yeltsin in the second round no matter what their leader did.[51] In fact, because Yeltsin did not need Yavlinsky to mobilize new voters in the first round (Yavlinsky, on the contrary, competed directly with Yeltsin's electoral base), the Yeltsin campaign would have preferred to remove the Yabloko leader as soon as possible.[52] As part of their strategy to marginalize Yavlinsky, Yeltsin's advisers pressured bankers and industrialists to refrain from supporting him. The Yeltsin team also made it impossible for Yavlinsky to appear on television because Yavlinsky's former ally in television, NTV, was now firmly on Yeltsin's side. The Yeltsin campaign also circulated disinformation about Yavlinsky, including rumors that Yavlinsky's campaign was financed by Sergei Mavrodi, the head of MMM, a notorious pyramid scheme in which millions of Russians lost money.[53] Finally, the Yeltsin team also tried to fuel divisions within Yabloko by actively courting the liberal wing of the party.

One month before the first ballot, Yeltsin suddenly offered Yavlinsky the post of first deputy prime minister in charge of economic reform, a job similar to the position Chubais held in the government before he was asked to step down in January.[54] Yavlinsky, however, demanded more, including the dismissal of virtually every senior official in the government and the naming of a new prime minister and his cabinet.[55] In the letter outlining his demands, Yavlinsky threatened Yeltsin, warning him that "As you well know, the mood and position of voters one month before this election is extremely shaky. And I am certain that without the support of the democratic opposition you will lose."[56] Yeltsin lamented Yavlinsky's stance, stating that "he wants too much."[57] The very act of the compromise, however, undermined Yavlinsky's credibility as the leader of the democratic opposition.

Stage Two: "The Lesser of Two Evils"

By April, the first campaign objective—establishing Yeltsin as the only viable candidate from the reformist camp—had been accomplished, as polls indicated that the election had become a two-person race. In its April 7 poll, the Foundation for Public Opinion (FPO) showed Zyuganov with 25 percent, Yeltsin with 21 percent, and Yavlinsky a distant third with 9 percent. Two weeks later, Yeltsin passed Zyuganov for the first time in FPO polling.[58] ROMIR's April poll also showed Yeltsin and Zyuganov in a dead heat, with 20 percent each. Polls conducted by the Institute of the Sociology of Parliamentarianism, however, showed a serious gap between the two leading contenders in April. But even these polls clearly indicated that Zyuganov and Yeltsin were the two front-runners.

Having consolidated the proreform group behind its candidate, Yeltsin's campaign now began to focus more on the so-called centrist vote.[59] Electoral patterns from previous elections had clearly demonstrated that the loyal reform vote alone could not produce a victory for Yeltsin, as roughly 20 percent of the electorate belonged to neither the hard-core reformist nor the hard-core opposition camp.[60] To win in the second round, Yeltsin had to win over an apolitical, less ideological, but more skeptical kind of voter.[61] Survey research had identified several important traits of these so-called centrists. First, these voters did not follow politics closely. Second, they were apolitical: they could not distinguish between a social democrat and a liberal. Third,

this kind of voter was generally dissatisfied with Yeltsin's regime and
the current state of affairs within the country. For instance, centrist
voters singled out crime, corruption, and the war in Chechnya as
negative developments under Yeltsin's rule but did not want to return
to communism. Although critical of aspects the new socioeconomic
system, these people had learned to live within Russia's market economy and generally preferred this new system to the old. Equally important, these voters feared the inevitable instability and turmoil that
would accompany any attempt to reverse the present course of reform.
At this late date in the transformation process, a communist "counter-
revolution" would mean prolonged conflict and possibly civil war, at
least so these voters believed.[62]

Finally, these voters were indecisive. In the December 1995 elections, the centrist vote gravitated to a new moderate opposition party
(such as KRO or Svyatislav Fyodorov), a nonideological centrist bloc
(such as Women of Russia), or one of the two dozen apolitical mini-
blocs that won just a fraction of the vote individually but together
totaled more than 15 percent of the vote. Because these voters likely
changed their minds between 1993 and 1995 (with the exception of
Women of Russia, these kinds of parties did not exist in 1993), they
might be persuaded to change again in 1996. Moreover, polling data
in December 1995 revealed that this centrist voter decided both to
vote and for whom less than one week before election day.[63] In the
estimation of the Yeltsin campaign, these were voters that could be
won back.

To capture these centrist voters, "stability" emerged as a central
theme. Yeltsin polls indicated that more people feared a political
"earthquake" if Zyuganov won than did if Yeltsin won.[64] Highlighting
continuity under Yeltsin, including even negative continuity, became
a principal objective of the campaign in the second stage.

On the stump, Yeltsin positioned himself as the guarantor of stability, continuity, and progress.[65] Speaking in Omsk in May, Yeltsin
promised that "I will not allow a civil war under any circumstances."[66]
Noting the electoral successes of other executives at the gubernatorial
and mayoral levels, Yeltsin's campaign emphasized that people were
tired of ideological battles and longed for calm and continuity.[67] A
week before the first round of voting, Yeltsin stressed that Russia did
not need any more revolutions.[68]

Similarly, in Yeltsin-sponsored television spots, people on the street talked about a whole array of problems in contemporary Russia. Each ended, however, by stating that it is better to stay with the present course than to change course in midstream.[69] In almost all forms of campaign communication, the term *course* featured prominently. Although the path Russia had started down in 1991 may have had many potholes and difficult stretches, Yeltsin's message stressed that the present course offered progress and a better life, while the alternative course—the communist path—offered more hardship, greater uncertainty, and possibly even violent conflict.

As discussed above, Yeltsin had to eliminate issues of instability to make this pitch credible, including first and foremost ending the war in Chechnya. Yeltsin, however, also highlighted positive developments of stability under his presidential leadership. At the end of March, for instance, he joined with the leaders of Belarus, Kazakstan, and Kyrghyzstan to sign the Union of Four agreement, a document that called for greater integration between these former Soviet republics and Russia.[70] Days later, in a lavish ceremony at the Kremlin, Russia and Belarus created the Community of Sovereign Republics, an even bolder step toward reintegration.[71] At both these events, Yeltsin emphasized the peaceful, gradual method in which his administration was pursuing integration in contrast to the confrontational approach preferred by the Communists. Yeltsin defended his so-called policies of disintegration in 1991 by arguing that the Belovezhkaya Pushcha Agreement (signed in December 1991) was the only way to avoid anarchy and civil war:

> The Belovezhk accords were necessary mainly to turn the former republics of the collapsing union back to the center, toward the idea of a new union, to stimulate the negotiation process, and most important, to avoid the bloody "Yugoslav scenario" of uncontrollable collapse not only of the Soviet Union, but also of Russia itself—since already in 1991 the USSR law of 26 April 1990 [which gave the ethnic republics inside the Russian Federation more autonomy—a move by the Soviet government to weaken the power of Yeltsin's Russian government] was already showing results in terms of the events in Tatarstan and Chechnya. Therefore it is strange to hear today that our actions were directed at the consensual collapse of the union and its immediate destruction. I know that it will not be easy to overcome this myth, but I emphasize

once again: the CIS [Commonwealth of Independent States] was the
only possible way of preserving a united geopolitical space at that time.[72]

At a summit in May, all CIS presidents publicly endorsed Yeltsin.[73]
Uzbek president Islam Karimov went to far as to say that Gennadii
Zyuganov is "completely unacceptable."

Yeltsin also capitalized on his international reputation to reinforce
the stability message. In May, Russia hosted for the first time a meeting
of world leaders from the G-7 countries. Although none of the visitors
to Russia directly endorsed Yeltsin, the message of the meeting was
clear: under Boris Yeltsin, Russia was a member of the club; under the
Communists, Russia would no longer be welcome.[74] Soon thereafter,
Yeltsin traveled to China for the first time to reaffirm his "presidentialism" and international standing in a communist country.

Strikingly, the development of Yeltsin's positive image in this campaign was distinctly nonideological and less aggressive than previous
campaigns.[75] If candidate Yeltsin in 1991 was portrayed as the champion of democracy, the fighter for individual rights, and the destroyer
of communism, candidate Yeltsin in 1996 ran more as a guarantor of
stability, the father figure above partisan politics. Although Yeltsin
aides drafted a comprehensive hundred-page platform, the campaign
ignored policy issues from Yeltsin's past term and proposals for the
future. Instead, campaign communications promoted generic, nonideological slogans such as I Believe, I Love, I Hope; Vote with the
Heart; and Yeltsin—the President of All Russians.

Negative Campaigning

The Yeltsin campaign contrasted these messages about stability with
subtle and not-so-subtle images of instability should Gennadii Zyuganov win. Throughout the campaign, and especially between the first
and second rounds, the Yeltsin campaign highlighted images of communist rule in Russia that included civil war, famine, repression, and
consumer deficits. Around the May 9 holidays celebrating the Soviet
victory over Germany in World War II, the Yeltsin campaign ran a
series of advertisements with veterans saying, "I just want my children
and grandchildren to finally savor the fruits of the victory we fought

for and that they didn't let us enjoy."[76] Other television advertisements emphasized the continuity between the CPSU and the present CPRF. One advertisement warned, while showing footage of executions, famine, and the destruction of churches during the Soviet period, "Russia's Communists have not even changed the name of their party; they will not change their tactics either." Anticommunist documentaries and the best and most famous anticommunist films accompanied these campaign spots on television, especially in the later stages of the campaign.

In print, the anticommunist message was everywhere. The Yeltsin campaign placed hundreds of anticommunist articles in national and regional newspapers. As mentioned above, the hardest-hitting anticommunist publication was a new newspaper called *Ne Dai Bog* (God forbid). The popular *Moskovskii Komsomelts* was also fervent, running anticommunist articles and cartoons daily in the final weeks of the campaign. In Moscow, campaign posters contrasted the empty shelves of 1991—Yeltsin's first year in office—with the stocked stores of 1996.

Recurrently, the Yeltsin team warned of impending violent conflict should the Communists lose the election.[77] Just two weeks before the first round, Yeltsin adviser Georgii Satarov warned that the Communists were planning to seize power by force before the election. Such statements cast the CPRF and its leader, Gennadii Zyuganov, as an antisystemic political force that refused to play by the democratic rules of the game. In March, the Communists aided in this task by voting in the Duma to renege on the Belovezhkaya Pushcha agreement, effectively declaring that the Soviet Union still existed and that Russia was not a legitimate state. The Yeltsin propaganda machine responded immediately, portraying the vote as tantamount to a declaration of war against Russia's neighbors. Baltic and CIS leaders denounced the vote in unison, helping Yeltsin look like the candidate of peace and Zyuganov the candidate of war.[78] The Yeltsin campaign also intimated that a Zyuganov victory would re-create a cold war confrontation with the West.

Understanding Yeltsin Pork

In addition to promoting the central message—stability under Yeltsin, instability under Zyuganov—Yeltsin used his powers as the incumbent to promise something to everyone.[79] Over the course of the campaign, the Yeltsin campaign targeted virtually every major constituency. In March, Yeltsin announced a dramatic new decree that promised to transfer the ownership of all state-owned farmland to the peasants and workers on state and collective farms, thus challenging the control of kolkhoz directors over state lands and rural votes. To appeal to the youth vote and their parents, Yeltsin announced in May his idea for having a professional army by the year 2000.

On the campaign trail, Yeltsin promised increased public spending in dozens of sectors and regions. To appeal to voters working at military enterprises, Yeltsin announced in May that funding for modernizing Russian military hardware would be increased.[80] Soon thereafter, his economic adviser announced that the government planned to dispense 800 billion rubles to cover May salaries in Russia's military-industrial complex.[81] Yeltsin met with a group of university rectors to pledge more money for universities and institutes. Two months later, First Deputy Prime Minister Oleg Soskovets announced that the government had allocated an additional 2.8 trillion rubles ($558 million) to eliminate teachers' wage arrears and to cover annual leave payments.[82] At a builders' meeting, Yeltsin pledged more credit for new family housing.[83] In a meeting with retired voters, Yeltsin promised to sign into law a raise of 10 percent in state pensions.

Yeltsin felt especially generous while traveling. In every city that he visited during the campaign—twenty-five in all—he made some kind of new commitment.[84] Most popular were power-sharing agreements that Yeltsin signed with several regions, including the oblasts of Irkutsk, Omsk, Rostov, and Sakhalin, the Ust-Orda Buryat Autonomous Okrug (AO), and the Republic of Chuvashiya. On signing these new agreements, Yeltsin underscored his achievements in building a new Russian federalism that provided "the kind of independence which they can handle . . . within the framework of the constitution."[85] Treaties were often accompanied by money or at least the promise of money. For instance, while in Omsk, Yeltsin signed a decree to establish a long-term federal program for the social and economic development of Siberia. Visiting Arkhangelsk in May, Yeltsin announced, "I've come with full pockets. . . . Today a little money will be coming into Arkhangelsk Oblast."[86] While in the city, the president signed decrees promising more state support for Arkhangelsk Oblast's social and economic development and instructing the government to approve a development program for small and medium-size towns within the next two weeks. The following day in Vorkuta, Yeltsin announced a 133-billion-ruble ($26.6 million) package of support for the Pechora coal basin, as well as a series of fringe benefits for miners and their families. As in every city visited by the president during the campaign, wages owed to Vorkuta miners arrived just days before Yeltsin's visit.

Some have argued that this slew of populist decrees produced Yeltsin's victory.[87] Tracing a direct causal relationship between increased spending and votes for Yeltsin, however, is empirically difficult to demonstrate.[88] Nor was government spending considered an effective campaign method by the Yeltsin campaign team. On the contrary, Yeltsin's campaign managers tried to limit the scope of the president's promises, believing that such statements raised expectations that could not be met and increased resentment in those regions not visited by the president.[89] These pledges did, however, buttress Yeltsin's new image as an active, hands-on president.

Resources and Allies

Yeltsin enjoyed a tremendous advantage in that, as mentioned above, he had the support of all major businesspeople, bankers, and industrialists in Russia, giving his campaign an unlimited budget.[90] Formally, several business organizations, including the Union of Bankers, the Union of Industrialists and Entrepreneurs, and the Union of Landowners endorsed Yeltsin, but informally every major corporation or bank in Russia backed the president.[91] This private money was bolstered by control over federal government spending, which Yeltsin audaciously manipulated for electoral benefit. An International Monetary Fund loan of $10 billion over three years, as well as a two-billion deutsche mark loan from Germany, both concluded in 1996, provided Yeltsin with the budget to pursue public spending projects.[92] The law on presidential elections did specify spending limits for the campaign, but everyone, including Yeltsin's own campaign team, agrees that the Yeltsin campaign grossly violated these restrictions.[93]

Yeltsin's most cherished campaign resource was his monopolistic control over all three national television stations. The European Institute for the Media estimated that those television networks—ORT, RTR, and NTV—devoted 53 percent of their election coverage time to Boris Yeltsin. Not only quantity but also quality of coverage mattered, as all three networks provided favorable coverage of Yeltsin's every move in contrast to critical coverage of Zyuganov.[94] Yeltsin also enjoyed support from most national newspapers as well as important regional publications. *Izvestiya, Trud, Kuranty, Argumenty i Fakti, Segodnya, Moskovskii Komsomolets, Kommersant'—Daily,* and *Vechernyaya Moskva* were all firmly behind Yeltsin.[95] Only *Sovetskaya Rossiya, Pravda,* and *Zavtra* were not.

Additionally, dozens of nongovernmental organizations, independent trade unions, and professional associations rallied to Yeltsin's cause. The remnant of the Soviet trade union structure, the Federation of Independent Trade Unions (FNPR), did not actively campaign for Yeltsin, but, most significantly, neither did it endorse Zyuganov. Some local FNPR branches did work closely with the Zyuganov campaign, but the neutralization of this natural communist ally at the national level was considered a major victory for the Yeltsin team.[96] The Russian Orthodox Church, along with several smaller churches and religious organizations, tacitly supported the president.[97] Even before Lebed joined the president's staff after the first round, Yeltsin had made inroads into the military vote when General Boris Gromov, the former commander of Soviet forces in Afghanistan, joined the Yeltsin campaign team in May.

Most regional governors and republican presidents also supported Yeltsin. Although once considered one of the most talented "red" governors, Yegor Stroyev, the chairman of the Federal Council, openly backed the president. Other electorally important endorsements came from Yurii Luzhkov, the extremely popular of mayor of Moscow, Eduard Rossel', the newly elected governor of Sverdlovsk Oblast, Primorskii Krai's governor, Evgenii Nazdratenko, Saint Petersburg's new mayor, Aleksandr Yakovlev, and Nizhnii Novgorod's Boris Nemtsov, a close friend of Grigorii Yavlinsky's who nonetheless sided with Yeltsin.

Yeltsin gained new support from the autonomous republics. Whereas most leaders of the autonomous republics had campaigned against the challenger Yeltsin in 1991, almost all the presidents of the autonomous republics endorsed Yeltsin the incumbent in 1996, though some with greater conviction than others. As discussed below, those republican presidents who produced only moderate support for Yeltsin in the first round of the election earned special attention from the Kremlin before the second round.

By the end of the first round, Yeltsin's team believed that its strategy had succeeded. By the end of April, Yeltsin had surged ahead of Gennadii Zyuganov in most opinion polls.[98] In June, Yeltsin's lead over Zyuganov was measured at 13 percentage points (35 to 22) in the Foundation for Public Opinion poll. No one was more optimistic about the campaign than Yeltsin. Appearing on NTV's weekly news program, *Itogi*, a week before the first round, Yeltsin predicted his victory in that round. So sure of himself was he that he claimed in the interview that he had prohibited his campaign team from making plans about the second round.[99]

4

The Zyuganov Campaign

Gennadii Zyuganov began the 1996 presidential campaign season with several major advantages over the other candidates. Most important, Zyuganov had behind him a genuine national political party. After a confused and poor showing in the December 1993 parliamentary elections,[1] the Communist Party of the Russian Federation (CPRF) leaders devoted tremendous energy to rebuilding and consolidating a grassroots political party with representatives in every city, town, village, and kolkhoz in Russia. Thus in the two years between the 1993 and 1995 parliamentary elections, the CPRF had developed a comprehensive program for party organization and development. The CPRF used its parliamentary resources (phones, faxes, office space, personnel, etc.) not to draft legislation but to develop the party outside parliament.[2] Additionally, CPRF leaders (first and foremost Gennadii Zyuganov) used their travel privileges as deputies to make extensive tours of Russia's regions. While Duma liberals flew to Paris and Washington, Communists took trains to Kursk and Bryansk. During this period, CPRF leaders reached out to new social groups and popular nonparty members of the opposition.[3] They reactivated the Komsomol, the communist youth wing, strengthened trade unions and women's groups sympathetic to the communist cause, and even began to court businesspeople who might benefit from a "stable" future under CPRF leadership.[4] Additionally, CPRF participation in local races between

1993 and 1995 served to test and mobilize local party organizations in preparation for the State Duma elections.[5]

This organizational work paid off. As demonstrated in its electoral victories on the national party list and its extremely strong performance in single-mandate districts in the 1995 parliamentary elections, the CPRF clearly had regained its pre-1993 position as Russia's premier opposition party. The CPRF's 1995 electoral victory endowed Zyuganov with a second major advantage: momentum. In Zyuganov's estimation, the 1995 results demonstrated that "anticommunist" sentiment, attributed to even by Zyuganov's allies, did not exist.[6] On the contrary, the results showed that the electorate had become more leftist during the last two years.[7] In January 1996, therefore, almost everyone, both in Russia and abroad, thought that Zyuganov would win a free and fair election in June. Even before the presidential campaign began, internal CPRF debates erupted over future portfolios in a Zyuganov government.

As a partial consequence of the CPRF's 1995 electoral victory, Zyuganov managed quickly to unite most parties and movements of the opposition behind his candidacy. Within his own party, Zyuganov convened a plenum soon after the 1995 elections to ensure that prospective challengers from within, such as Aman Tuleev or Pyotr Romanov, had no opportunity to organize.[8] On winning the nomination from his own party, Zyuganov then turned to the left, gaining an early endorsement from the Union of Communist Parties and a reluctant stamp of approval from the militant Russian Communist Workers' Party (RKRP), headed by Viktor Tyulkin and Viktor Anpilov.

With his communist base secured, Zyuganov then reached out to leaders and groups of Russia's nationalist opposition. Under the leadership of former Soviet prime minister Nikolai Ryzhkov, Zyuganov helped create the Bloc of National and Patriotic Forces, a coalition of nationalist and communist organizations. By the end of the campaign, an alleged 136 organizations had registered their support for Zyuganov and his bloc.[9] Well before the campaign began, Zyuganov had persuaded such nationalist leaders as Aleksandr Rutskoi, Sergei Baburin, and Stanislav Govorukhin to join the bloc because, without the Communists at this stage in Russia's political development, no patriotic movement was possible.[10] (Zhirinovsky was the only major figure from the nationalist camp that was not invited to join.) For the first time in five years, Russia's "reds" and "browns" were united. Early in the campaign period, then, Zyuganov established himself as the focal candidate of the opposition.

Zyuganov's third and final advantage entering the presidential campaign was the competition. As discussed above, Yeltsin had single-digit approval ratings at the beginning of the campaign. Yeltsin's first term also offered the Zyuganov campaign several issues to exploit. In particular, public opinion polls confirmed that most Russians felt that they had been better off under communism than under the present economic system.[11] Besides Yeltsin, none of the other candidates posed a serious threat in a two-ballot system, and polls showed that both Aleksandr Lebed and Grigorii Yavlinsky could defeat Zyuganov in a runoff. These same polls, however, also indicated that none of these candidates had a chance of making it to the second round. Ironically, then, Zyuganov and Yeltsin had a shared interest in keeping this election polarized between two choices.[12] According to Zyuganov, "centrism" had collapsed in the December 1995 elections and would do so again in the presidential race.[13]

Reaching to the Middle

With his base consolidated early in the year, Zyuganov's campaign began addressing how to reach out to new voters.[14] Theoretically, Zyuganov had two choices. Like his comrades in East-Central Europe, he could try to recast himself and his party as social democrats, hoping to mobilize new voters through left-of-center social policy issues. Or he could try to position himself and his campaign as nationalists, reaching out to new voters through nationalist, patriotic slogans rather than through bread-and-butter issues.

In reality, Zyuganov chose the nationalist strategy well before the 1996 presidential campaign.[15] During the creation of the Russian Communist Party in 1990, Zyuganov had emerged as one of the leaders of the statists (*gosudarstveniki*). After the Soviet collapse, Zyuganov found new ideological allies and mentors in Aleksandr Prokranov, the editor of the hard-hitting nationalist newspaper *Den'*, and Aleksei Podberezkin, a former intelligence official who founded Spiritual Heritage, a think tank devoted to nationalist causes.[16] Throughout the heady

confrontational politics of 1992–1993, Zyuganov was the most promi-
nent Communist to assume a leadership role in the Front for National
Salvation (FNS), the then leading nationalist opposition movement.
In his speeches and writings during this period, Zyuganov emphasized
imperialist, nationalist, and patriotic themes, only rarely mentioning
Marxism-Leninism or socialism.

The decision, then, of whether to create a national patriotic bloc
or a social democratic movement was an easy one for Zyuganov. As he
argued when asked to explain this decision, "In Russia, social democracy of the West European type has no chance."[17] CPRF leaders, in
fact, emphatically rejected the social democratic label.[18] Thus the Zyuganov campaign devoted little effort to courting Russia's nascent social
democratic parties or trade unions. Strikingly, and in sharp contrast
to most leaders of leftist parties in postcommunist Europe, Zyuganov's
electoral platform and stump speeches were devoid of social democratic themes.[19]

According to their interpretation of the Russian electorate, patriotic slogans could produce victory, perhaps even in the first round.
Zyuganov and his advisers believed that Russian voters consisted of
three types in relatively equal proportions—democrats, Communists,
and nationalists.[20] If Zyuganov could win support from the latter two,
he would win. As Zyuganov proclaimed, "Two-thirds of Russian voters
support the idea of national patriotism and social equality."[21]

Zyuganov's strategy for capturing this nationalist middle paral-
leled Yeltsin's dual approach—paint Yeltsin as destabilizing and gen-
ocidal while portraying himself and his ideas as new and pragmatic.
Zyuganov tried to make the vote a referendum on Yeltsin's tenure. On
the campaign trail, Zyuganov emphasized the "bankruptcy of the anti-
people [antinarodnii] regime."[22] According to Zyuganov, Yeltsin had
waged an economic war against his own people:

> There have been attacks on our territory. We have repulsed them all,
> but the most recent incursion has qualitatively different characteristics.
> People armed with lies, slander, and fraud came to us, as if they were
> trustworthy and honest, promising to lead us to civilization, but in reality
> destroying all the most important institutions of the Russian state. In-
> dustry is being destroyed. When the Fascists were near Moscow, the
> drop in production was 24 percent. Now it has fallen by more than 50
> percent.[23]

When speaking in cities, Zyuganov criticized the total destruction of the Soviet military-industrial complex and the continuing decline of industrial production, the neglect of science and education, and the "criminal" process of privatization under the Yeltsin regime.[24] In the countryside, Zyuganov lambasted Russia's declining agricultural production and the lack of state support for rural areas.[25] In Zyuganov's estimation, the ultimate consequence of this set of policies was genocide. According to CPRF deputy chairman Valentin Kuptsov, 53.2 million Russians were living below the poverty line.[26] Under these conditions, "it is not possible to improve one's life under the present regime."[27] Summing up the incumbent's tenure, Zyuganov stated that "Yeltsin's five-year period [ended] with a devastated economy, the war in Chechnya, and a global extinction of Russia's population."[28]

To counter Yeltsin's predictions of civil war should a Communist win the election, Zyuganov frequently noted that Yeltsin already had instigated a war in Chechnya that could easily spread throughout the rest of Russia.[29] Zyuganov also cited rampant corruption within the Yeltsin government and escalating crime in society as further signs of instability. More generally, Zyuganov labeled Yeltsin and his team immoral, decadent, and unpatriotic. In Zyuganov's view, Yeltsin served the interests of the United States and Western capitalism, not the Russian people or Russian values.[30]

Zyuganov offered a more palatable, stable alternative to the Yeltsin regime. The message of one of his first television appearances was stability and moderation. As summarized by OMRI:

Communist candidate Gennadii Zyuganov used his free advertising time on 27 May on Russian Public TV (ORT) to emphasize the moderate aspects of his career. The advertisement shows the candidate with his family and talking to the camera in an informal setting. . . . He does not discuss his party leadership or ties with nationalist organizations. Zyuganov blames the collapse of the USSR and the Communist Party of the Soviet Union on the "monopoly on power, truth, and property" that the leaders then wielded. However, he salutes the middle-level managers who continue to work in spite of society's current problems. He pledges to support everyone willing to work, regardless of their party membership. . . . He says that he is ready to cooperate with everyone, including the president and government, to guarantee political stability.[31]

To promulgate this image of moderation, Zyuganov's campaign began criticizing its own allies. Valentin Kuptsov, the head of Zyuganov's campaign, categorically denounced all forms of extremism, including "leftist-Trotskyite methods and ultrapatriotism."[32] Instead, Zyuganov's campaign platform portrayed himself and his movement as "the responsible opposition."[33] Regarding the extreme left, Zyuganov denounced the so-called Maximum Plan, a secret blueprint for rolling back the market drafted by communist radicals. Zyuganov also expressed disappointment in the March 15 Duma resolution that called for the abrogation of the 1991 Belovezhkaya Pushcha accord, lamenting privately that the language of the resolution was too radical.[34] On the campaign trail, Zyuganov emphasized that he was the leader of a national patriotic bloc, not the Communist Party of the Russian Federation.[35] His campaign rhetoric reflected this ideological migration; he rarely uttered terms like *communism, socialism,* or *Marxism-Leninism.* This tack apparently paid off, as polls showed that 40 percent of Russia's voters had negative feelings towards Communists compared with Zyuganov's personal negative rating of 23 percent.

To distance himself from the radical right, Zyuganov took special aim at Vladimir Zhirinovsky. In CPRF campaign literature, Zhirinovsky was portrayed as a collaborator with Yeltsin's "party of power."[36] Kuptsov declared that Zhirinovsky was as bad if not worse than the current regime.[37] Despite numerous rumors about cooperation between Zhirinovsky and Zyuganov, especially after the first round, Zyuganov rejected the notion entirely. Although denouncing Zhirinovsky personally, Zyuganov nonetheless courted former Zhirinovsky supporters. Recounting the results of the December 1995 elections, Zyuganov explained that Zhirinovsky's electorate consisted of unfortunate, disenfranchised people who had lost their political orientation and were therefore susceptible to Zhirinovsky's demagoguery.[38] Before the presidential ballot, Zyuganov made it one of the CPRF's central tasks to help these people "find" their true political orientation.

When speaking about specific issues, however, Zyuganov's moderate message became garbled.[39] On economic issues, Zyuganov at times (especially when abroad) tried to sound accepting of the market.[40] Speaking at the World Economic Forum in Davos, Switzerland, for instance, Zyuganov spoke approvingly of capitalism, welcomed Western investment, and promised to respect contracts and private property rights. At home, however, Zyuganov's economic message emphasized state intervention, regulation, and protectionism. Citing CPRF legislative initiatives regarding the minimum wage, pensions, education, salaries for servicemen, and new fringe benefits for families with children, Zyuganov promised greater state support for the economically disadvantaged.[41] Zyuganov also promised to use the state to stimulate industrial production, including state subsidies to the military-industrial complex and other high-tech industries.[42] Although recognizing that all forms of property should be legal, the Communist Party program clearly stated that "social forms of property will dominate."[43] Zyuganov's campaign program sought to "democratize relations of ownership," which meant a greater management role for worker collectives in all forms of ownership.[44] Moreover, Zyuganov explained that the sale of property was not part of Russian tradition and would lead to social unrest.[45] Zyuganov's economic message was extremely anti-Western. He and his aides constantly warned about the dangers of International Monetary Fund dictates, foreign investments, and the international pressures on Russia to become a raw materials exporter instead of an industrial power.[46] As for the market generally, Zyuganov often pointed out that an "underregulated market has never existed and never will."[47] In a refrain from early Soviet policies, his election platform called for support to peasants, including parity of prices between industrial and agricultural production.[48] Echoing Lenin, Zyuganov's electoral program called for a "state monopoly of foreign trade of natural resources and products of 'strategic significance' . . . as well as . . . preserving in state hands the most important branches of industry, energy, transport, and communications for the support of stable development and security."[49] Some of his allies even suggested that ration cards might have to replace free prices to guarantee a basic minimum bundle of goods for all.[50]

On the state, Zyuganov's message also was mixed. Regarding Chechnya, Zyuganov stated categorically that the war must end immediately as a "military solution in Chechnya does not exist."[51] At the same time, no one in the Zyuganov campaign advocated Chechen independence. On the contrary, they aimed to rebuild the entire Soviet Union, not dismantle Russia. Regarding other state-building issues, Zyuganov's campaign called for constitutional amendments that would grant greater power to the legislative branch of government and less autonomy to the presidential office.[52] His party's program also advocated more-radical changes including reinstating the system of soviets, as well as granting greater governing power to trade unions and workers' self-government so that "workers can more actively and more widely participate in the management of the affairs of the state."[53]

Regarding foreign policy, Zyuganov's campaign rhetoric echoed nationalist slogans from liberation movements in the Third World in the 1950s and 1960s.[54] As stated in the CPRF party program, "The CPRF puts forth the task to activate the national-liberation struggle of the Russian people."[55] Zyuganov's own election platform declared that the "The Fatherland is in danger! It is necessary to liberate national and state independence from the compradorial class" and "halt the extinction of Russia."[56] Several of Zyuganov's top deputies, including Chairman of the Duma Security Committee Viktor Ilyukhin, spoke frequently of an American plot to destroy the territorial integrity and industrial base of Russia.

Zyuganov's attitudes toward the history of Soviet communism also revealed his militant proclivities. Zyuganov spoke proudly of the continuity between his Russian Communist Party and the Communist Party of the Soviet Union. When pressed about Stalin, Zyuganov was not afraid to claim the dictator as a hero of his party whose horrible exploits were grossly exaggerated. Zyuganov refrained from endorsing the criticisms of Stalin from the CPSU's historic Twentieth Party Congress and even stated on American television that Stalin had *only* killed 600,000 people, not the several millions cited by most historians.[57] At the same time, Zyuganov admitted that many communist leaders, including Stalin, abused power and made mistakes. In his reinterpretation of history, there had always been two factions within the CPSU:[58] one was the party of Trotsky, Khrushchev, Gorbachev, and Yeltsin, and the other was the party of Stakhanov, Gagarin, and Andropov. His party, course, was the successor to the latter faction.[59]

Obstacles to Victory

Was Zyuganov a moderate, a conservative, a nationalist, or a Communist? To voters unequivocally opposed to Yeltsin and his policies, these labels mattered little. Well before the campaign began, these voters had decided to vote for Zyuganov. To other more-moderate voters, however, these debates—or images of these debates—did matter. Zyuganov's greatest electoral challenge was to keep his core supporters mobilized by spouting militant discourse, while at the same time attracting centrist voters through more moderate rhetoric. Unfortunately for Zyuganov, the national television networks highlighted Zyuganov's appeals to the faithful and failed to broadcast his remarks aimed at the centrists. At the same time, radicals such as Viktor Anpilov enjoyed more national television time during the campaign than ever before.

The ideological contradictions in Zyuganov's message reflected the political struggles within his opposition bloc, which ultimately may have been too broad in scope to run an effective campaign. Debate within the bloc was most acute regarding economic issues. Zyuganov considered the first draft of his economic program, written under the direction of Yurii Maslyukov, too extreme; after more moderate economists composed a second draft, however, radicals within the bloc protested. Eight drafts later, Zyuganov finally published an economic program that sounded much more militant than the candidate.

Debate about cooperation with other political forces also occupied the time and energy of the Zyuganov campaign. To keep the radicals on board, Zyuganov publicly praised such militants as General Varennikov, Viktor Anpilov, and Stanislav Terekhov. (At one point, Zyuganov even suggested that Anpilov might be appointed the head of ORT television in a Zyuganov government.)[60] Later in the campaign, however, Zyuganov tried to downplay his contacts with these militants and their ideas. This ideological waffling produced a crisis within the bloc. At a special secret plenum of the CPRF, Zyuganov was urged by his party's leadership, who had began to worry that Zyuganov was alienating the hard-core opposition, to adopt more decisive and communistic language in his campaign speeches.[61] Toward the end of the campaign, as discussed below, several militant communist and nationalist groups finally denounced Zyuganov as an opportunist and urged their supporters to boycott the election.

These internal debates within Zyuganov's national patriotic bloc also impeded negotiations with political personalities and parties outside the electoral coalition.[62] For instance, moderates within Zyuganov's campaign saw cooperation with Third Force presidential candidates Svyatoslav Fyodorov, Aleksandr Lebed, and Grigorii Yavlinsky as vital for victory in the second round. Communist Party deputy chairman Aleksandr Shabanov suggested that people from all these political organizations would be welcome in a Zyuganov government.[63] Radicals in Zyuganov's camp, however, opposed any cooperation. Late in the campaign, Zyuganov invited all three candidates to join him, but because the offer was for capitulation, not cooperation, they declined.[64] Negotiations with Zhirinovsky also never happened, though the LDPR leader had hinted early in the campaign that he might join in a patriotic alliance with Zyuganov.

In many ways, Zyuganov's individual presidential bid was similar to the CPRF's collective parliamentary campaign. Decisions were made by committee, not by the candidate and his campaign staff. Strong personalities within the party seemed to be campaigning for themselves, not for their candidate. For instance, Aman Tuleev, allegedly one of Zyuganov's most important backers, spoke openly about joining a Yeltsin postelection government only days before the second round of the election was over.[65] Zyuganov failed above all to project an image or style of his own, choosing instead to stay behind the cloak of the collective. When campaigning, he usually used the pronoun "we," not "I," in discussing beliefs and policy issues. Although appropriate and effective for the party vote in the parliamentary elections six months earlier, presidential campaigns all over the world tend to focus more on personalities than programs. Thus keeping Zyuganov's personality hidden behind an amorphous portrait of his party proved ineffective. It also made Zyuganov an easy target for Yeltsin's negative messages about Communists and communism.

Communist Campaign Technology

Developing an effective campaign message was not the only problem for Gennadii Zyuganov; communicating that message proved equally troublesome. On one level, Zyuganov enjoyed several organizational advantages: The CPRF boasted the only genuine, grassroots party organization in Russia. Through its five hundred thousand members, the CPRF could distribute campaign material faster and more widely than any other party. At the top of this rich network of regional offices and local activists sat Zyuganov's campaign headquarters, located at the State Duma. In January, the CPRF Duma faction "lent" deputies to the Agrarian and Power to the People factions, allowing them to reach the threshold (thirty-five deputies) to register.[66] In so doing, the CPRF controlled 221 votes of the 226 needed for a simple majority, which allowed the CPRF to assume tremendous control over the Duma, both as a legislative organ and as a source of state-funded resources for the campaign.[67]

Second, although Zyuganov's bloc endured several ideological struggles, his campaign did not suffer the same splits that plagued the Yeltsin camp. Valentin Kuptsov, the head of Zyuganov's campaign, enjoyed universal respect; as the former chief of staff for the CPRF Duma faction, the number-two person in the CPRF leadership (after Zyuganov), and the leading organizer within the party, his authority helped create a disciplined party. Zyuganov received strategic and ideological advice primarily from Dukhovnoe Nasledie (Spiritual heritage), the nationalist think tank run by Aleksei Podberezkin; Russian Scientists of Socialist Orientation (ROSO), headed by Ivan Osadchii; and a team of writers and philosophers working with Aleksandr Prokhanov, the editor of *Zavtra*. All reported to Zyuganov directly, and never during the campaign did splits between these groups erupt. Under the professional leadership of Nikolai Ryzhkov, the seventy organizations constituting the National Patriotic Bloc also effectively coordinated their activities with the candidate and his immediate advisers.[68]

This organizational capacity provided Zyuganov with a powerful weapon of agitation. To take advantage of this resource, the campaign relied primarily on printed material as a method of communication.[69]

Likewise, the party machine organized all Zyuganov's public appearances on the campaign trail. So confident were Zyuganov's campaign advisers in their grassroots organization that they rarely purchased local radio or television time. At the national level, Zyuganov only attempted to buy national time on July 1, one day before the official end of the second round. ORT general director Sergei Blagovolin blocked the application, saying it had arrived too late. That the first request for airtime came only hours before the end of the campaign, however, demonstrates the low priority assigned to this method of campaigning.

More generally, Zyuganov and his campaign team adopted a hostile attitude toward the press, believing that it would only report negative news about their campaign. The Zyuganov campaign thus devoted little energy or resources to public relations, and Zyuganov's press office was the last to know about its candidate's activities. That office released little information about the campaign and was generally unhelpful to Russian journalists assigned to write about the communist campaign.[70]

Not all Zyuganov's problems in dealing with the press were of his own making. The experience with buying ORT airtime reflected the tremendous obstacles Zyuganov faced. As noted above, all national television networks openly opposed Zyuganov, making it virtually impossible for him to stimulate positive news coverage.[71] According to campaign organizers, even local television and radio refused to sell time to the CPRF.[72] In the regions, most executive leaders either opposed Zyuganov or were instructed by the Kremlin to refrain from assisting him. Business, of course, feared Zyuganov and his comrades, making it difficult for the campaign to raise money. The Yeltsin government actively encouraged directors of large enterprises, military commanders, and other employees of the state to avoid contact with CPRF campaigners. Nonetheless, "red" directors did provide funds quietly to the Zyuganov campaign, but this support was only a fraction of that pledged to the Yeltsin team.[73]

Internal ideological divisions, outdated campaign technologies, and aggressive state opposition combined to limit the effectiveness of Zyuganov's presidential campaign. Throughout the campaign season, Zyuganov's ratings never improved (see table 3). Although CPRF internal polls were more optimistic, even CPRF campaign officials

Table 3   Support for Zyuganov (in percent)

Polls	February	March	April	May	June
All-Russian Center for the Study of Public Opinion (VTsIOM)	24.0	25.0	26.0	26.0	24.0
Foundation for Public Opinion (FPO)	16.4	25.8	28.0	22.4	

believed that Zyuganov faced a ceiling of potential support ranging from 25 to 30 million votes. As demonstrated in previous elections, most of these loyal supporters of Zyuganov were likely to vote, unlike Yeltsin's supporters, who were unenthusiastic about their candidate. To win, then, Zyuganov had to reach this ceiling and hope for a low voter turnout.

5

The Rest of the Field

The winner-take-all vote and Russia's polarized electorate quickly shaped Russia's presidential election into a two-person race. By April, opinion polls placed Yeltsin and Zyuganov several percentage points ahead of the rest of the field. At the same time, these polls indicated that anywhere from a third to a half of all voters planned to vote for a third-party candidate. Such large numbers kept alive the possibility that a united Third Force could advance to the second round,[1] for voters who supported third-party candidates in the first round would ultimately decide who won in the second round. Understanding these voters and their preferences, therefore, was vital to both the Yeltsin and Zyuganov campaigns.

Early in 1996, opinion polls showed that most voters did not like either Boris Yeltsin or Gennadii Zyuganov. Such sentiments sparked intense speculation about the electoral potential of a Third Force. Proponents of this idea argued that a coalition of non-Communists and non-Yeltsin supporters could defeat either Zyuganov or Yeltsin in a runoff. To make a serious challenge, Third Force advocates called for a united bloc headed by Grigorii Yavlinsky, Aleksandr Lebed, and Svyatoslav Fyodorov.

Although none of these three presidential candidates originated the Third Force idea, all recognized its logic.[2] Running individually, none stood a chance of advancing to the second round; in the December 1995 parliamentary elections, Yavlinsky garnered the most support of the three with 7 percent of the vote. United, however, these three popular leaders believed that they could retain their combined support from the 1995 elections of 15.5 percent and then win the amorphous centrist vote (roughly 20–25 percent). Even if they won only half the centrist vote, the Third Force candidate would be propelled into the second round. In a runoff, polls showed that either Yavlinsky or Lebed could defeat Yeltsin or Zyuganov.

Which two, though, would withdraw as candidates and support the third? Third Force supporters discussed several mechanisms for resolving this problem, including primaries and public opinion ratings. When those methods did not win support from any of the principals, it was left to bargaining between the candidates. Throughout the spring, several indicators suggested that Yavlinsky and Lebed were close to a deal. Earlier in the campaign, Yabloko had assisted Lebed in collecting signatures. Yavlinsky and Lebed then met several times, much more frequently than either met with Fyodorov.

In May, however, the loose coalition fell apart. As became public later, Yeltsin and Lebed had already agreed to a deal in April. (In retrospect, Lebed's flirtation with the Third Force after April may have been an effort to distract the other presidential hopefuls.) Yavlinsky also consulted with Yeltsin about cooperation, which Lebed charged was a betrayal of their gentleman's agreement.[3] Without Lebed, an alliance between Fyodorov and Yavlinsky had no meaning.

Aleksandr Lebed

Of the three candidates, Lebed ran the most successful campaign and then used that success to propel his own political career. Unlike the other Third Force candidates, Lebed did not hesitate to seek an alliance with Yeltsin. Even before the campaign season began, several Yeltsin allies had approached the retired general to discuss possible forms of cooperation. In March, as discussed above, Lebed communicated through intermediaries his desire to meet with Aleksandr Korzhakov, at the time one of Yeltsin's closest advisers. After their meeting in April, Lebed informally agreed to support Yeltsin if the general was given (1) the green light to raise money from Yeltsin's backers and (2) a prominent post in Yeltsin's postelection government. Allegedly, Lebed expressed particular interest in the post of minister of defense. Yeltsin reconfirmed his commitment to Lebed in May, when the two held a series of discussions. Later in the campaign, Yeltsin even hinted that Lebed was his choice for his successor:

> There is a need to prepare a future president whom people know, who has authority, and who is loved by all Russians. I know such a person, and in his case I would withdraw my candidacy. In that case for sure, he would be elected president next time around.[4]

For Yeltsin, the alliance was a brilliant campaign move. By staying in the race to the end, Lebed would attract voters who would never have voted for Yeltsin in the first round. With Lebed in the Kremlin after the first round, these voters might cast their support behind the Yeltsin-Lebed ticket. The deal also meant that Lebed would not co-operate with Yavlinsky. For Lebed, the deal was also too attractive to refuse, for it gave him the opportunity to compete actively in the first round of the campaign, assured him of a postelection political career, and propelled him to the front of the pack of potential successors to Yeltsin. With no financial or organizational resources and little campaign experience, Lebed had struggled even to register. Once he had an agreement with Yeltsin, Lebed had a new opportunity to run an effective campaign.

After leaving the Congress of Russian Communities, Lebed formed his own political group, Chest i Sovest (Trust and conscience), which assumed primary responsibility for his presidential campaign.[5] Although this disciplined and organized group of mostly retired military officers proved capable of collecting one million signatures with virtually no financial resources, Lebed realized that his loyal and dedicated soldiers were not qualified to run a national campaign. Aleksei Golovkov, a Duma deputy, founder of Our Home Is Russia, and acting Prime Minister Yegor Gaidar's former chief of staff, also realized that Lebed needed help. In April, Golovkov approached Lebed with an offer to run his campaign. When Lebed accepted, Golovkov put together an experienced team of campaign strategists, speech writers, and television specialists that completely revamped the Lebed campaign.[6] Because of his informal agreement with Yeltsin, Lebed received financial backing from the same banks and entrepreneurs that had backed Yeltsin, with special assistance coming initially from Oneksimbank and Inkombank.[7] More important, the deal with Yeltsin gave Lebed a green light to appear on national television networks, an advantage that no other challenger to Yeltsin enjoyed. Armed with a professional campaign team, money, and access to the national media, General Lebed entered this election in a much stronger position than he had been in during his first electoral experiment in December 1995.[8]

Lebed's campaign message was simple but effective. As a general untainted by past political or ideological struggles, Lebed used populist slogans to promise law and order. Truth and Order became the banner of his campaign. In his literature and on the campaign trail, Lebed promised to crack down on crime on the streets and corruption in the government, stealing campaign themes away from Vladimir Zhirinovsky.[9] Unlike Zhirinovsky, however, Lebed's campaign messages lacked imperial thirst. He categorically objected to the war in Chechnya, and many of his paid television advertisements emphasized antiwar themes. One, for instance, featured Lebed saying, "I know war, and I know that war must be stopped." Another Lebed leaflet argued that "the weak carry out wars. The strong do not allow wars to happen." Lebed also emphasized the need to eliminate corruption within the military and reform the army more generally. As for the near abroad or other foreign policy issues, Lebed's campaign, unlike Zhirinovsky's or Zyuganov's, did not trumpet pro-Soviet or anti-Western messages. Guided by polling data and his personal concerns, Lebed focused instead on issues closer to home.

Regarding economic issues, Lebed broadly supported the current *course* that Russia was on, a code word that everyone understood as support for market reforms. Lebed, however, remained deliberately vague about his positions on specific economic issues. As the publication of two contradictory economic platforms indicated, Lebed understood little about economics but much about economic issues that influence electoral politics.[10] Although unable to wax on about macroeconomic stabilization, he frequently stated that people who worked must be paid for their labor.[11]

Lebed's campaign style, image, and delivery were as important as the message itself. His witty, flippant responses to questions produced made-for-television sound bites. His written campaign materials contained jingoistic, populist slogans that resonated with voters tired of both Yeltsin and the Communists. For instance, in ridiculing Defense Minister Grachev's optimism about a quick victory in Chechnya, Lebed's campaign leaflets declared that "In Chechnya, indeed, we should have fought with one regiment: a regiment of Kremlin (leaders') children." Lebed gave equal time to scorning communist ideas.[12] In reference to a popular idea that Russia needed to adapt Sweden's model of socialism, Lebed responded, "Of all 'Swedish models,' only the 'Volvo' is appropriate for us." To emphasize his pragmatic, non-ideological character, Lebed asserted, "Those who see Russia in red-white colors should get their eyes fixed." Lebed's giant build, baritone voice, and provincial looks added force and authenticity to these clever idioms.

Grigorii Yavlinsky

Yavlinsky's presidential bid suffered its greatest setback in the 1995 parliamentary election, when Yabloko won only 7 percent of the popular vote. Although winning almost seven hundred thousand more votes in 1995 than in 1993, Yavlinsky's share decreased by nearly a full percentage point between elections, hardly a solid launch for a presidential bid.[13] Because of his poor showing in 1995, potential financial backers, liberal parties, and reformist leaders lost confidence in Yavlinsky as a viable presidential candidate. Yeltsin's team, by orchestrating a comprehensive anti-Yavlinsky strategy, compounded Yavlinsky's troubles. Yeltsin supporters at Russian television stations executed a media boycott that included NTV, a channel once sympathetic to Yavlinsky's cause. The Kremlin also discouraged Moscow's financiers from supporting Yavlinsky. Even Most Bank's Vladimir Gusinskii, a longtime backer of Yavlinsky, supported Yeltsin in this election. Similar pressure was applied to regional leaders to the extent that Nizhnii Novgorod governor Boris Nemtsov, Yavlinsky's longtime ally and friend, endorsed Yeltsin, not Yavlinsky. Finally, Yeltsin's team fueled division within Yabloko, while encouraging futile negotiations between Third Force leaders and between Yeltsin and Yavlinsky.

If these external conditions severely constrained Yavlinsky's ability to run effectively, strategic decisions made by Yavlinsky equally damaged the campaign effort. Yavlinsky's first mistake was to isolate his campaign from the Yabloko Party organization, making it clear to his Yabloko colleagues that his presidential bid was a personal campaign, not a party issue.[14] The party helped collect signatures to register Yavlinsky but then participated only in the margins during the remainder of the campaign. In place of his party organizers, Yavlinsky hired a team of professional consultants from Saint Petersburg. Although successful in winning a single-mandate seat for Yabloko faction member Pyotr Shelesh in 1995, these consultants had no national campaign experience.[15] It showed.

Yavlinsky's second mistake was failing to articulate a clear, compelling campaign message. To get to the second round, Yavlinsky had to convince the core reformist voters that he was the only genuine reformist alternative on the ballot and that Yeltsin was a traitor to the liberal, reformist cause. Polls showed that Yavlinsky was the preferred candidate of these voters but that these voters were reluctant to waste their vote on a nonviable candidate.[16] Yavlinsky received important endorsements from liberal leaders such as Sergei Kovalev, Yelena Bonner, Yurii Afanasiev, and Arkadii Murashev, which enhanced his case.[17] Within Democratic Choice of Russia and other smaller liberal parties, debate continued throughout the spring about whether to support Yavlinsky or Yeltsin.

Ultimately, however, Yavlinsky failed to articulate a clear message. Much of Yavlinsky's campaign, in fact, was devoid of any message at all. Yavlinsky's paid television advertisements were best described as silly, featuring babushkas in the countryside singing jingles about Yavlinsky that contained no political message whatsoever. The dissonance between these lighthearted spots of singing farmers and Yavlinsky's own serious, intellectual, urban persona was apparent to even the casual observer.[18]

Through other mediums, the Yavlinsky campaign tried to communicate that Yavlinsky was the candidate of the "democratic opposition," but these messages were too abstract. For instance, many of Yavlinsky's posters and leaflets carried the slogan I Choose Freedom. Focus group work indicated, however, that voters did not understand the message. Yavlinsky's position against the war in Chechnya was clear, but Yeltsin's peace initiative diluted its salience.[19] On economic reform, Yavlinsky suggested that his approach to privatization would be more equitable and his policy toward social policy more supportive of the disadvantaged. He also promised to raise the minimum wage three times in six months and double the average government salary, pension, and stipend.[20] Nothing in Yavlinsky's campaign materials, however, was strikingly different from the economic policies of other challengers to Yeltsin. In sum, Yavlinsky failed to give voters a compelling reason to vote for him.

Svyatoslav Fyodorov

When the buzz surrounding the Third Force ended, so too ended Svyatoslav Fyodorov's moment in the limelight. Similar to his strategy in 1995, Fyodorov's modest campaign effort portrayed a pragmatic man with business and organizational experience. The eye surgeon's campaign advertisements tried to appeal to centrist, nonideological voters. His campaign had one original idea: employee ownership. As Fyodorov explained:

> I am a realistic socialist, a democratic socialist, in favor of something like people's capitalism. I want all people to become small capitalists in their country, so they have their own home, capital.[21]

This message, however, did not resonate. In Russia's polarized electoral setting, a rich capitalist who advocated collective ownership had no political niche.

Vladimir Zhirinovsky

From the outset of the campaign, Vladimir Zhirinovsky and his advisers knew they had little chance of advancing to the second round.[22] Zhirinovsky's objectives in this election were more modest: to win roughly the same percentage as the LDPR collected in 1995 (11 percent), place third in the first round, and thereby avoid extinction as a presidential contender in future elections.[23] Early in the campaign Zhirinovsky and his team realized how difficult reaching his 1995 showing would be.

Zyuganov's resurgence as the new leader of the hard opposition coupled with Lebed's effective campaign crowded the field for populist, opposition candidates like Zhirinovsky. To succeed, Zhirinovsky and his campaign strategists concluded that they could not repeat LDPR campaign strategies from previous elections.

Zhirinovsky's first new strategy, then, was to avoid participating in the election. Zhirinovsky first tried to cut a deal with either Yeltsin or Zyuganov before the first round. In doing so, Zhirinovsky hoped to survive as a national political figure, while winning portfolios in the powerful executive branch. Throughout the campaign, Zhirinovsky offered his support to both sides. In June, Zhirinovsky announced that he would back Yeltsin, in return for being named minister of propaganda in Yeltsin's postelection government,[24] and threatened to join the Communists after the first round if Yeltsin did not accept his offer.[25] At the same time, Zhirinovsky attempted to cut an alliance with Zyuganov and Lebed whereby Zyuganov would be president, Zhirinovsky prime minister, and Lebed defense minister.[26] Neither Zyuganov nor Yeltsin seriously considered an alliance with Zhirinovsky. (Within Yeltsin's campaign, Aleksandr Korzhakov advocated such an alliance, but Yeltsin rejected the idea.)[27] For some in Zyuganov's national patriotic bloc, however, an alliance with Zhirinovsky made ideological and electoral sense.[28] Zhirinovsky's parliamentary antics, however, had alienated too many CPRF leaders including Zyuganov himself to make such a deal possible.

Zhirinovsky's other strategy in this election was to try to position himself as the "centrist" between Yeltsin's radical democrats and Zyuganov's radical Communists.[29] Television commercials and Zhirinovsky stump speeches consistently emphasized this centrist line: First Russia had tried communism, then democracy, and now it was time to try a third way, Zhirinovsky.

This centrist rhetoric did not tame Zhirinovsky's radical anti-Western racist positions or alter the LDPR's leader's outlandish behavior. Zhirinovsky continued to lambaste the West for first destroying and then occupying Russia, to accuse Caucasians of most crimes in Russia, and to ridicule both the Communists and Yeltsin for outdated ideas and bankrupt politics.[30] On the campaign trail, Zhirinovsky tried to appeal to communist supporters, praising the work of rank-and-file members of the party but lambasting their leaders.[31] To appeal to this group of voters, Zhirinovsky openly promoted Russian imperialism and praised Stalin as a great Soviet leader.[32] Evidently, in Zhirinovsky's view, this nationalist rhetoric did not contradict his centrist message.

Zhirinovsky's campaign appeared to be financially well endowed, as only Yeltsin and Lebed outspent him on television advertisements.[33] Hundreds of LDPR newspapers, leaflets, and pamphlets also were distributed throughout Russia, demonstrating that the LDPR had built a vast network of grassroots political organizations, second only to the Communist Party in reach. Zhirinovsky, however, did face the same obstacles to receiving television exposure as other opposition candidates.[34] Unlike previous campaigns, Zhirinovsky's stunts and antics did not receive media coverage, positive or negative, in this race.

Mikhail Gorbachev and Others

The other candidates played little or no role in the election. Gorbachev occasionally appeared on television, but no one (including his campaign managers) considered him a contender.[35] The millionaire Vladimir Bryntsalov attracted attention by replicating Zhirinovsky's theatrics. He and his flamboyant wife, who at one point dropped her skirt before television camera crews, made news by being outrageous but attracted few votes. Martin Shakkum's clever television spots made his campaign visible, but no one took him seriously as a candidate. The campaign run by former Olympic weight lifter Yurii Vlasov was invisible.

6

The Homestretch

First-Round Results

As expected, Yeltsin and Zyuganov captured significantly more votes than any of the other candidates (see table 4). The small margin separating the two front-runners, Lebed's strong third-place showing, and Zhirinovsky's demise were the most noteworthy results of the first ballot. These outcomes also helped shape strategies in both the Yeltsin and the Zyuganov camps between rounds.

Yeltsin's Second-Round Strategy

Despite his predictions of a first-round victory, Yeltsin's campaign leaders were more cautious. Yeltsin won the first round, however, if only by 3 percentage points. In winning 35 percent, Yeltsin's total was 5 to 10 points below polling predictions but not much below numbers estimated within the campaign. (Had Yeltsin placed behind Zyuganov, advocates of postponing the second round would have been in a stronger position.) Yeltsin campaign managers then reasoned that the close margin would help mobilize proreformist voters for the second round.[1] If Yeltsin had won by a landslide in the first round, his supporters might not have bothered to show up for the second round.

Table 4   First-Round Results

	Percentage	Total Votes (in millions)
Turnout	69.81	75.7
Yeltsin	35.28	26.7
Zyuganov	32.03	24.3
Lebed	14.52	11.0
Yavlinsky	7.34	5.6
Zhirinovsky	5.70	4.3
Fyodorov	0.92	0.7
Gorbachev	0.51	0.4
Shakkum	0.37	—
Vlasov	0.20	—
Bryntsalov	0.16	—

For results by region, see the appendix.

Lebed placed a strong third, just as Yeltsin's team wanted. The general's late campaign blitz helped him secure almost a third of those voters who made their electoral choice only days before.[2] Zyuganov did not widen his electoral base; in the first round, he won roughly the same level of support that the CPRF, the Agrarians, and Anpilov's radical Communists had won in 1995. Momentum was on Yeltsin's side.

Some aspects of the first-round voting disappointed the Yeltsin campaign. Yeltsin's percentage share in several republics and a few oblasts was below expectations (see table 5).[3] The Yeltsin campaign team did not worry about the disappointing results in oblasts such as Arkhangelsk, Murmansk, Vladimir, and Ivanovo, for these were places where Lebed pulled votes away from Yeltsin, and the Yeltsin team calculated that these voters would come back to Yeltsin in the second round. Yeltsin's support in Tatarstan, Dagestan, and Ingushetiya, however, was more alarming as these were places where local leaders were supposed to influence the results in favor of Yeltsin and yet they did not vote any differently than their oblast neighbors. In the Northwest, the Republics of Karelia and Komi demonstrated strong support for Yeltsin at levels similar to their neighbors in the oblasts of Murmansk and Arkhangelsk. In contrast, in the Volgo-Ural region, Tatarstan and Bashkortostan voted like their neighbors, giving Zyuganov a slight

Table 5   Regions in Which Yeltsin Placed below Expected Results
               by 5 Percent or More

Region	Yeltsin Expected	Yeltsin Actual	Difference
Arkhangelsk	47	42	−5
Chuvashiya	26	21	−5
Dagestan	40	26	−13
Ingushetiya	75	46	−29
Irkutsk	38	33	−5
Ivanovo	38	30	−8
Kostroma	33	28	−5
Marii El	31	25	−6
Mordoviya	30	25	−5
Murmansk	46	41	−6
Novosibirsk	31	26	−5
Tatarstan	51	35	−16
Vladimir	37	31	−6

edge. Republics in the northern Caucuses also voted like the contiguous oblasts in the region, rejecting Yeltsin and supporting Zyuganov.[4] With 2.7 million voters, reversing the results in Tatarstan was deemed especially important compared with the less populous republics.

Nationwide, voter turnout was 5 to 8 percentage points below what Yeltsin's team had anticipated. According to its own survey data, the youth vote did not turn out as well as expected; many more danced at the Vote or Lose concerts than voted.

These first-round results dictated the tasks and tactics of the second round.[5] Most immediately, Yeltsin carried out his plan with Lebed.[6] On June 18, two days after the first-round voting, Yeltsin appointed Lebed to serve as both the president's adviser on national security and as the secretary of the Security Council, with newly extended powers over the Ministry of Defense and the Ministry of Internal Affairs. In satisfying one of Lebed's preconditions for the deal, Yeltsin fired his defense minister, Pavel Grachev. This dismissal was discussed throughout the campaign, as public opinion polls showed that Grachev's resignation would help Yeltsin considerably with undecided voters.[7] Days later, Lebed dismissed seven more top generals close to Grachev, asserting that they were plotting a putsch against the government.[8]

Lebed never formally endorsed Yeltsin or urged his voters to cast their support for Yeltsin. On the contrary, he stated that "I don't trade people who have entrusted me with their votes."[9] He also made clear that he supported neither the reds nor the whites, who were polarizing Russian politics. He claimed that his voters had opted for a third way, a path of "social accord and a civil society where differences in incomes and different ideological commitments don't turn people into enemies."[10] In joining Yeltsin's government, Lebed wanted to signal that he was his own man, with his own popular following.

Although Lebed's appointment heightened uncertainty about the balance of power within the Kremlin, his alliance with Yeltsin virtually assured Yeltsin's victory in the second round. The photos of Lebed and Yeltsin together in the Kremlin were more important than any verbal endorsement of Yeltsin's candidacy. Many observers originally assumed that Lebed and his voters would support Zyuganov during the runoff.[11] In analyzing Lebed's electoral victory region by region, however, it became clear that Yeltsin was better placed than Zyuganov to win over Lebed's supporters.

Lebed won almost eleven million votes, or 14.5 percent, of the total vote in the first round of the presidential race, eight million more votes than he and his electoral bloc, the Congress of Russian Communities, won in December 1995. When analyzed region by region, we see that Lebed captured a large portion of his new voters from Mr. Zhirinovsky. Especially in the Far East, there was a direct correlation between Lebed's success and Zhirinovsky's defeat.[12] So why would Zhirinovsky supporters vote for Yeltsin in the second round? Polls carried out by the Foundation for Public Opinion in January 1996 indicated that Zhirinovsky's electorate consisted of two types of voters:[13] Half his electorate resembled the demographic profile of Communist Party supporters—rural, poor, and alienated from the new market system. These voters probably supported Zhirinovsky again in 1996 and were unlikely to vote for Yeltsin in the second round. An almost equal percentage of Zhirinovsky supporters in 1995, however, were affluent, lived in medium-sized cities, supported market reform, but were not satisfied with the Yeltsin regime. This kind of voter most likely abandoned Zhirinovsky in 1996 in favor of the new Third Force, Alexander Lebed, and would never vote for a Communist. With Lebed in the Kremlin, Yeltsin campaign officials predicted that these voters would either stay home or reluctantly vote for Yeltsin.

Not all Lebed's supporters, however, came from Zhirinovsky. Again, a regional comparison of the June 16, 1996, results with the December 1995 parliamentary elections reveals that Lebed also picked up new support from both the so-called democratic opposition vote and the amorphous centrist, or "swamp," vote. For instance, Lebed performed above his national average in 1996 in several areas in which Yavlinsky had done well in 1995 including Rostov, Murmansk, Yaroslavl, Chelyabinsk, and Saint Petersburg. In these reformist-oriented regions, Lebed won votes away from Yavlinsky as well as consolidated the centrist vote that had been dissipated among dozens of small electoral blocs in 1995. Especially after Lebed joined forces with Yeltsin, these voters were likely to support Yeltsin in the second round.

Moreover, there was little evidence to suggest that Lebed actually took votes from the Communists, a claim made loudest by communist backers.[14] On the contrary, even with a 5 percent increase in turnout, the communist vote remained stable between 1995 and 1996 both as a national aggregate and on a region-to-region basis. Lebed made no inroads here.

Polls conducted between rounds also confirmed the anticommunist and pro-Yeltsin orientation of Lebed backers in the runoff. The Mitofsky International/CESSI exit poll conducted on election day revealed that 44 percent of Lebed's supporters planned to vote for Yeltsin in the second round and that only 34 percent planned to back Zyuganov. According to a between-rounds poll conducted by VTsIOM, 57 percent of former Lebed voters planned to support Yeltsin in the second round compared with only 14 percent for Zyuganov.[15] The Foundation for Public Opinion reported similar results.[16] More generally, two-thirds of all Russians thought that Yeltsin made the right decision in bringing Lebed into his government.[17]

Yeltsin and his campaign team also courted Yavlinsky but with less vigor. Polling data suggested that three out of four Yavlinsky supporters who planned to vote in the second round would support Yeltsin, even if Yavlinsky was not a member of the team. As expected by Yeltsin's aides, Yavlinsky and Yabloko could not commit to backing Yeltsin. Between rounds, Yabloko held a national conference to decide whom to endorse in the second round. Yavlinsky decided not to address the conference or express his personal inclinations. Without leadership from the top, the Yabloko regional delegates carved out a convoluted position in which they urged their supporters *not* to vote for Zyuganov, *not* to vote for none of the above, but they did not encourage voters to support Yeltsin.[18] Frustrated with Yavlinsky's wavering, Chubais openly criticized the Yabloko leader, saying that he had "exhausted his moral right to enter the government."[19]

Between the first and second round, Yeltsin set up several meetings with Yavlinsky but canceled all of them. Whereas Lebed had translated his electoral victory into a major new Kremlin job and thereby ensured a future for his presidential aspirations, Yavlinsky won nothing in his negotiations with the president. As he lamented soon after the first round, "I have become the president's hostage."[20]

The Yeltsin team did not openly court Zhirinovsky, as its polls concluded that Yeltsin would lose 17 percent of his electorate if he openly allied with Zhirinovsky.[21] At the same time, it had hoped for a tacit Zhirinovsky endorsement. He delivered it in a dramatic and emotional press conference in which he ridiculed Zyuganov and his allies for claiming to be nationalists when it fact they were unreformed Communists. For LDPR loyalists, Zhirinovsky sent a clear message: Do not vote for Zyuganov.

A second task of the Yeltsin campaign between rounds was to reverse its poor showing in Russia's republics. Kremlin officials sent clear signals to republican leaders concerning the consequences of not delivering the vote, eliciting quick responses from several of Russia's key republics. In Tatarstan, President Shaimiev tacitly instructed state officials to ensure the "proper" electoral support for Yeltsin in the second round. Those who had not produced the right result in the first round, including the deputy premier for agricultural affairs, were dismissed between rounds. In Dagestan, Yeltsin's representatives tapped so-called authorities (local mafia bosses) to mobilize the vote for the president.[22] A popular cosmonaut from Dagestan also campaign on Yeltsin's behalf between rounds. In Bashkiria, President Murtaza Rakhimov gathered local executive heads and threatened to dismiss those who did not deliver good numbers for Yeltsin in the second round.[23]

The third priority for the Yeltsin campaign between rounds was voter turnout. As discussed above, polls showed conclusively that the

greater the turnout, the more likely Yeltsin would win.[24] Most analysts
predicted that turnout would decrease in the second round; this was
a common pattern in other countries with two-ballot systems and was
confirmed in Russia during local elections. For Yeltsin, the timing of
the second round—a Sunday in the middle of summer—could not
have been worse, as rich, urban dwellers (i.e., Yeltsin supporters)
traveled to their dachas on July weekends. The Yeltsin campaign addressed the turnout problem in three ways: First, it changed the date
of the second round to Wednesday, July 3, to ensure that Yeltsin voters
would be in town. Second, the Central Electoral Commission conducted a massive television campaign to get out the vote. Third, the
Yeltsin campaign increased the volume of anticommunist television
commercials to scare people into voting.

Scandal

Between rounds, the Yeltsin campaign team had planned several mobilization tactics and events.[25] Yeltsin was slated to travel to Nizhnii
Novgorod, Samara, and Tula, and the campaign had hoped to send
Lebed to the southern regions of Stavropol, Rostov, and Krasnodar to
appeal to nationalist voters.[26] Additionally, two pieces of direct mail
were prepared and a series of "democratic" congresses were planned
to convene throughout the country on the weekend before the vote.[27]
All these activities and several other minor events were canceled, however, because of Yeltsin's poor health and the eruption of internal
battles within the campaign.

Between the first and second round, Yeltsin did not campaign at
all. He did not travel outside Moscow, and his television appearances
consisted solely of scripted and heavily edited pieces. Not until well
after the end of the campaign did we learn that Yeltsin had suffered
another heart attack between rounds and was thus unable to carry out
his planned campaign agenda.

The Yeltsin campaign was further derailed by an internal crisis
that erupted just three days after the first round of the election, when
two of Chubais's aides were detained for questioning by Federal Security Service (former KGB) officers for taking $500,000 in cash from
the prime minister's office.[28] Korzhakov sought to use the incident to

undermine Chubais and his team. Throughout the campaign period, Korzhakov and his allies had advocated postponing the election. In March, after the Duma had voted to reunite the Soviet Union, Korzhakov's postponement scenario was rejected by Yeltsin. In May, Korzhakov worked with a group of powerful bankers, the Group of Thirteen, to issue a plea for postponement. These bankers called on Yeltsin and Zyuganov to unite and form a coalition government so that competitive elections could be avoided. As Boris Berezovskii, one the signers of the Group of Thirteen letter, stated: "The question is not whether or not to postpone the elections. The problem is finding a legal way to do it. Either we find a compromise or we have civil war."[29] In June, a bomb blast in Moscow's metro was interpreted by many as the pretense Korzhakov would use to crack down on the opposition and postpone the elections.[30] Throughout the campaign, Korzhakov's analytic center fed Yeltsin forecasts about his electoral prospects that were much more pessimistic than the assessments made by Chubais's team.

After the first-round results, Yeltsin's victory and Chubais's newly acquired influence over the president were obvious to all in the campaign. Realizing that a Yeltsin victory produced by Chubais would significantly diminish Korzhakov's power in the Kremlin, Korzhakov had struck preemptively against Chubais and his colleagues.[31] When Chubais heard of the detentions, he (apparently with Chernomyrdin's support) gave Yeltsin an ultimatum: either fire the so-called party of war responsible for the "harassment" or Chubais and his entire campaign team would resign. Yeltsin concurred with his daughter (who also pushed strongly for Korzhakov's ouster) and Chubais and dismissed Aleksandr Korzhakov, head of Presidential Security and a close personal adviser and friend for more than a decade: Mikhail Barsukov, director of the Federal Security Service; and First Deputy Prime Minister Oleg Soskovets.

No one knew how this Kremlin intrigue would influence second-round voting. One the one hand, Yeltsin had proven yet again his decisiveness and willingness to revamp his government. On the other hand, the reemergence of the unpopular Chubais from behind the scenes to center stage would not help Yeltsin. Others feared that the instability in the Kremlin also would hurt Yeltsin's reelection chances. Several rock concerts associated with the Vote or Lose (renamed between rounds Vote and Win) took place, Central Election Commission get-out-the-vote plugs appeared relentlessly on all national television stations, and a hard-hitting anticommunist paid advertisement aired continuously as well. On the whole, though, Yeltsin's campaign was much less active leading up to the second round of voting than it had been in the days before the first round.

Zyuganov's Second-Round Strategy

Publicly, Zyuganov expressed delight with the first-round results. Despite Yeltsin's media blitz and lavish spending, the president's showing equaled that of Zyuganov. In Zyuganov's reading of the first-round results, two-thirds of the population voted against the incumbent.[32] As for his own performance, Zyuganov pointed out that he placed first in forty-two subjects of the federation and won more than 50 percent of the vote in eleven regions.[33]

When the cameras and microphones were off, however, campaign officials were not as cheery about the first-round results.[34] Zyuganov's first-round showing was not a surprise to his campaign organizers, as even their polls had indicated that Zyuganov's support had leveled off early in the campaign. Although the June results were a bit higher than polls projected, the actual vote total for Zyuganov had not changed appreciably after six months of campaigning. In 1995, the Communist Party, the Agrarians, Anpilov, Rutskoi, and Ryzhkov combined for 24 million votes; in the first round of the presidential election, Gennadii Zyuganov won 24.2 million votes.[35]

To analysts both in and out of the Zyuganov campaign team, the first-round results demonstrated that Zyuganov had failed to win any new voters beyond the hard-core opposition. As Igor Bunin, director of the Centre for Political Technologies, concluded, Zyuganov's "failure in the first round was in not deemphasizing the communist identity."[36]

What did surprise Zyuganov and his campaign was Yeltsin's strong first-round showing. Zyuganov, like many other noncommunist analysts, had assumed that Yeltsin would perform several points lower in the actual vote than his polling numbers predicted. Speaking on the eve of the first round, campaign director Valentin Kuptsov revealed that their internal research showed Zyuganov's support at 29 percent, with Yeltsin 12 points lower at 17 percent.[37] Kuptsov and his associates guessed Zyuganov's support accurately but grossly underestimated Yeltsin.

Polls about Zyuganov's runoff prospects also were not encouraging. The CNN/*Moscow Times* and VTsIOM polls showed Yeltsin outdistancing Zyuganov by 20 percentage points if turnout in the second round did not decline appreciably.[38] The Foundation for Public Opinion called the race closer, giving Yeltsin 50 percent and Zyuganov 46 if the turnout reached 65 percent, but many speculated that this poll, coming from the presidential campaign's chief pollster, might have been falsified to stimulate voter turnout. No matter which poll one believed, the Zyuganov campaign realized that victory in the second round was highly unlikely.[39]

This lack of optimism perhaps explains why Zyuganov virtually stopped campaigning after the first round. Between rounds, he never once traveled outside Moscow. Even within Moscow, the CPRF convened only one major public event and Zyuganov made only a few appearances before live audiences. As mentioned earlier, his campaign also did not purchase television time or devote significant resources to new printed materials. In fact, his campaign spent well below the mandated limits.

Zyuganov's only major campaign event during this period was a daily press conference designed to get him on the evening news every night. Zyuganov devoted most of these press conferences to discussions of his coalition government. Zyuganov's campaign team reasoned that Zyuganov had to move to the center between the first and second rounds, to "become more pink."[40] Assembling a coalition government with noncommunist and centrist members, therefore, seemed like a fast and effective way to reposition Zyuganov. In his first announcement, Zyuganov stated that one-third of such a coalition government would come from his national patriotic bloc, one-third from the sitting government, and one-third from the remaining political forces. When asked for specific names, Zyuganov stated that presidential candidates Svyatoslav Fyodorov and Grigorii Yavlinsky; the mayor of Moscow, Yurii Luzhkov; Prime Minister Chernomyrdin; and regional leaders Vitalii Mukha (Novosibirsk), Murtazy Rakhimov (Bashkortostan), Yegor Stroyev (Orlov), and Eduard Rossel (Sverdlovsk) would all be welcome.[41] Even after Lebed's deal with Yeltsin, Zyuganov continued to court the general, telling him he could assume an even greater role in a Zyuganov government.[42] (Conspicuously absent from Zyuganov's list were hard-liners such as Anatolii Lukyanov, Valentin Varennikov, and Viktor Anpilov.)[43] Evidently, however, Zyuganov had not consulted with any of the moderate political leaders about their participation, as all of them rejected his offer.[44] Zyuganov spent the next few days after his announcement explaining these defections and denunciations.

As expected by Zyuganov's campaign team, his attempt to move to the center and his gestures of rapprochement with sitting government officials seriously strained his opposition coalition. Radicals on both the left and the right denounced him as a sellout, and, not surprisingly, Russian television devoted extensive coverage to the these denunciations, including long interviews with the neofascist leader Stanislav Terekhov from the Union of Officers and the neo-Stalinist leader Nina Andreeva.[45] Even more damaging, however, was the television interview with Aman Tuleev on the eve of the election in which the number-two leader in Zyuganov's electoral bloc talked openly about the possibility of joining Yeltsin's government after the election.[46] If Zyuganov could talk to Chernomyrdin about forming a coalition government, Tuleev reasoned that he had the right to pursue his own career interests.

To establish his centrist credentials, Zyuganov also met with several noncommunist leaders and organization between rounds, including a press conference with a group of unidentified "religious" leaders at which Zyuganov renounced Marx's disdain for religion and confessed that he was a "believer" of sorts. On the free television time provided, Zyuganov tried to project an image of a family man with a modest, rural background. There were no references to Marxism-Leninism, communism, or socialism in these television spots.

In the final days, the Zyuganov campaign tried to attack Yeltsin and his new ally, General Lebed. In one of Zyuganov's free television slots, Aleksandr Rutskoi denounced the Yeltsin-Lebed alliance as a plot to fool nationalist and patriotic voters and predicted that Lebed's career would follow his tragic tenure in the Kremlin as Yeltsin's vice president. Articles published in procommunist newspapers warned voters not to be fooled by Lebed's machinations.[47] Zyuganov and his team also ridiculed the dramatic changes in Yeltsin's entourage as signs of corruption and instability in the Kremlin[48] and tried to point out that the winner in this Kremlin struggle was Anatolii Chubais, the unpopular head of privatization who had "robbed the masses" of their property rights.[49] As mentioned earlier, Zyuganov's campaign also tried to buy television time on ORT to feature a short film, produced by Stanislav Govorukhin, that criticized Yeltsin's drinking habits and questioned his health. (ORT officials, however, never aired the piece.)[50] Zyuganov continued this line of attack in his press conferences, suggesting that Yeltsin was unfit to rule. To prove his vigor and underscore the president's weakness, Zyuganov kept up active physical schedule during the last days of the campaign, including a televised volleyball match with his comrades and dancing at a famous rock disco. Zyuganov consistently challenged Yeltsin to a televised debate and then portrayed Yeltsin's refusal as yet another sign that the president was not healthy.[51]

Ultimately, Zyuganov's only hope for victory depended on voter turnout. If Zyuganov reached his maximum level of support, estimated by his own campaign team at about thirty million, he could win if turnout fell to 55 percent in the second round. Once turnout reached more than 60 percent, however, Zyuganov's team knew that he had no chance of winning.

Second-Round Results

Turnout in the second round was an amazing 69 percent, delivering to Yeltsin a landslide victory (see table 6). Yeltsin performed extremely well in Moscow and Saint Petersburg, where he outpaced Zyuganov by 50 percentage points! Yeltsin also performed extremely well in his traditional stronghold in the Urals. The northern European regions also gravitated back to Yeltsin in the second round. In Murmansk and Arkhangelsk, two regions in which Yeltsin performed 5 points below expectations in the first round, he defeated Zyuganov by more than 30 percentage points in the second round. In these northern regions, as well as in the Far East, Yeltsin's alliance with Lebed appeared to have been significant in changing the outcome between the first and second round.[52]

Table 6   Second-Round Results

	Percentage	Total Votes (in millions)
Yeltsin	53.82	40.2
Zyuganov	40.31	30.1
Against all	4.83	3.6
Turnout	68.89	74.7

For results by region, see the appendix.

An even more dramatic turnaround occurred in the republics. In Tatarstan, President Mintimer Shaimiev fired his deputy prime minister for agriculture, an alleged communist sympathizer, after the first round and then sent out a clear signal to all local authorities that he expected a strong show of support for Yeltsin. The overwhelming shift in support for Yeltsin between rounds in Tatarstan was beyond belief: Yeltsin won 64 percent of the vote there compared with 30 percent for Zyuganov.[53] In Dagestan, local officials also changed their endorsement between rounds, giving Yeltsin an electoral victory in a republic that had voted strongly for communist candidates in all previous elections. (Given the history of previous votes in this republic, falsification probably contributed to this dramatic turnaround. Likewise, the results in neighboring Chechnya were falsified in favor of Yeltsin.)

When contrasted with the results of the 1991 presidential elections, the electoral outcome in Russia's republic reveals a different dynamic than in the rest of Russia. In these republics, loyalty to the "party of power" has proven paramount. Powerful, clan-based networks headed by republican presidents continue to "organize" the vote. In 1991, republican leaders mobilized their electoral machines to support Nikolai Ryzhkov, the proximate representative of the party of power at that time. In contrast, Yeltsin, the challenger, performed very poorly in most republics (see table 7) even though he had promised republican heads greater autonomy should he be elected.[54] In 1996, Yeltsin represented the party of power and Zyuganov was the challenger. Again, most republics rallied behind the incumbent (see table 7).

As expected, the rural-urban divide helped determine the second

Table 7   Yeltsin Support in the Republics, 1991 versus 1996

| | SUPPORT FOR YELTSIN | | |
Republic	1991	1996	Growth
Adegiya	52.1	34.5	−17.6
Altai	22.4	43.0	20.6
Bashkortostan	45.9	51.0	5.1
Buryatiya	34.5	45.3	10.8
Dagestan	65.9	53.1	−12.8
Ingushetiya	76.7*	79.8	3.1
Kabardino-Balkariya	63.9	63.6	−0.6
Kalmykia	31.1	70.3	39.2
Karachaevo-Cherkassiya	61.8	49.9	−11.9
Karelia	53.3	66.2	12.9
Komi	47.6	64.4	16.7
Marii El	51.4	40.7	−10.7
Mordovia	61.6	45.6	−16.0
Sakha (Yakutia)	44.9	64.7	19.8
Northern Ossetia	27.3	43.0	15.7
Tatarstan	45.0	61.5	16.5
Tyva	15.2	63.1	47.8
Udmurtiya	51.9	52.8	0.9
Kakassiya	53.0	47.2	−5.8
Chechnya	76.7*	73.4	−3.3
Chuvashiya	52.3	31.8	−20.5

*At the time, Chechnya and Ingushetiya were one republic. This figure is the aggregate percentage for both places.

round of the presidential vote. Yeltsin won eighty-six out of Russia's hundred largest cities (which constitute 40 percent of Russia's electorate), receiving 63 percent of the vote from these urban centers.[55] Zyuganov defeated Yeltsin in thirty-one regions and maintained his strong support in the "red belt," where he outdistanced Yeltsin by 15 percentage points in eight oblasts. He did not make significant gains, however, in Siberia or the Far East, populist regions that Zyuganov campaign managers had hoped might either support Zyuganov in the runoff or at least not vote for Yeltsin. When Zyuganov's support is analyzed at the *rayon* level, we see that he failed to make inroads into the urban population. Strikingly, even in the red belt, Yeltsin defeated

Zyuganov in every capital city. The urban-rural divide has remained firm throughout Russia's electoral history.

The usual covariates with the urban-rural divide appeared again in this vote. As in earlier Russian elections, age served as a good indicator of voting behavior. VTsIOM polls in June showed a distinct age gap between Yeltsin and Zyuganov (see table 8).[56] Similarly, level of education correlated positively with those voting for Yeltsin (see table 9).[57] Finally, income level and support for Yeltsin were also positively correlated, though the gap between the two candidates at middle and lower levels was not large (see table 10).[58] In sum, the demographics of the second round of the 1996 presidential elections mirrored electoral patterns in Russia for the past six years. There were no surprises.

Zyuganov won thirty million votes, more than any communist leader in any national race in Russia's brief postcommunist electoral history. By most accounts, including his own campaign's internal assessments, Zyuganov achieved nearly the maximum level of support possible, given his chosen campaign strategy. Even in the euphoric month of January, no one in the Zyuganov camp predicted that an opposition candidate could win more than thirty million votes.

Falsification

Falsification or intimidation of voters did occur in this election. In the republics of Tatarstan, Dagestan, and Kalmikiya, Zyuganov's dramatic decline in support between rounds can only be explained by the active intervention of state officials, be it stuffing ballot boxes or threatening local officials to deliver the correct vote count. Moreover, when

Table 8   Age as an Indicator of Voting Behavior (in percent)

Age	For Yeltsin	For Zyuganov
18–24	58	5
25–39	40	15
40–54	30	26
55 and older	30	44

Table 9   Education as an Indicator of Voting Behavior (in percent)

Level of Education	For Yeltsin	For Zyuganov
High	45	55
Middle	38	20
Low	31	38

analyzed at the *rayon* level, there is tremendous variation in contiguous electoral districts with similar demographic and socioeconomic features. For instance, in Kalmikiya, two electoral districts reported that Yeltsin had won more than 87 percent of the vote in the first round, higher than any district in reformist strongholds such as Moscow or Saint Petersburg.[59]

Despite the apparent evidence of irregularities, neither Zyuganov nor anyone from the communist opposition challenged the election results. Zyuganov accused Yeltsin of "an unprecedented mobilization of state funds" for his personal electoral gain but never once accused his administration of fraudulent behavior.[60] After the second round, he congratulated Yeltsin, attended his inauguration, and then guided his Duma faction in approving Yeltsin's new government.

All electoral experts in Russia agreed that the ten-million-vote gap between Yeltsin and Zyuganov was too great to have been forged, overshadowing the relative minor instances of falsification. Before the first round, CPRF leaders pledged to field 200,000 election monitors.[61] Retrospectively, however, CPRF officials recognized that they did not have the organizational capacity to do a parallel vote count.[62] Although thousands of CPRF members did watch polls, the party did not establish an efficient, centralized system for accumulating their field reports. Moreover, after the first round, CPRF campaign officials were so convinced of defeat, be it through the ballot box or through force,

Table 10   Income as an Indicator of Voting Behavior (in percent)

Income level	For Yeltsin	For Zyuganov
High	54.8	16.5
Middle	33.3	29.9
Low	29.2	29.2

that they perceived a court challenge to the election result would be futile.

Explaining the Vote: A Recap

To summarize, three factors ultimately determined this electoral outcome: Russia's polarized electorate, the institutions of a presidential election, and the campaign strategies of the major candidates. Russia's polarized electorate is the one variable that has remained relatively constant throughout Russia's recent electoral history. One major issue has divided the country into two camps for the last eight years: those for "reform," however defined, and those against. In the late 1980s advocates of reform challenged the status quo; opponents of reform defended the status quo. In 1996, advocates of reform were the defenders of the status quo and opponents to reform now challenged the present order. As William Zimmerman stated in a report on his major survey of Russian voters after the second round of the presidential elections: "The vote in the second round of the 1996 presidential election was a referendum on the political system. Social scientists are never going to be more sure of a finding than about this."[63] Throughout Russia's electoral history, these two positions have shaped electoral behavior in every national election. The numbers and preferences of centrist voters between these two positions have changed over time, but the basic contours of the Russian electorate have remained stable.

Elections have produced such varying outcomes, not because of shifting voter attitudes, but because the kind of elections has changed and the strategies employed by candidates have varied. The causal relationship between type of election and electoral outcome is striking: presidential elections and referenda increase bifurcation and clustering of voters into two camps; parliamentary elections do not. The rules of the game governing the 1995 parliamentary elections provided few incentives for consolidation or cooperation between ideological allies. In contrast, the 1996 presidential election (like presidential elections throughout the world) did provide such incentives.

Russia's polarized electorate and the bipolar nature of presidential elections established the parameters of the possible in Russia's 1996 presidential election. Yeltsin could only win, however, if he selected the appropriate strategy for dealing with these societal and institutional constraints. Above all, this optimal strategy included (1) running as the candidate of reform, rather than as a Communist or nationalist, (2) marginalizing competitors on the reformist ledger, and (3) convincing voters that the costs of changing the status quo were much greater than the costs of continuing with the present course. In making this case, Yeltsin also had to prove that he was physically able to govern.

Yeltsin's own personal role in reshaping his image and campaign should not be underestimated. It was Yeltsin who stopped drinking, lost weight, began to interact with crowds, and turned toward the reformist pole both strategically and within his own entourage. As Yegor Gaidar commented,

> Yeltsin won because he is the best campaigner in Russia. . . . In 1994 and 1995 everybody forgot that he knows how to win election campaigns. But more than anyone else, he knows how to talk to Russian people, to dance with Russian people, and to deal with Russian people.[64]

A different strategy—a strategy that did not take into account the effects of societal and institutional polarization—would have produced a different outcome. For instance, had Yeltsin tried to position himself on the other side of the ledger and run as a Communist or nationalist, he would have opened the door for another candidate to capture the reformist vote. Had Yeltsin allowed Lebed, Yavlinsky, or even Chernomyrdin to emerge as a serious candidate during the 1995 parliamentary elections or the early stages of the presidential race, he might not have emerged as the focal point of the reformist vote. Finally, had Yeltsin run a more confrontational, "revolutionary" campaign, similar to his first presidential race in 1991, he may have alienated those "centrist" voters who above all else wanted stability and continuity.

Regarding this last calculation, Zyuganov's choice of campaign strategies greatly assisted the Yeltsin effort, as Zyuganov's fiery rhetoric about Russian nationalism and Soviet communism frightened away the centrist voters. Retrospectively, several of his aides and allies lamented the fact that Zyuganov did not run as the leader of a loyal opposition but felt compelled to run as the champion of the revolutionary opposition. His campaign platform and speeches were often more radical than his own personal positions.[65] As CPRF Duma deputy Vladimir Semago commented: "We . . . shifted too far to the left. We must take more centrist positions."[66] After the campaign, Zyuganov quickly broke ranks with both nationalist and communist radicals and formed a new organization, the National Patriotic Union of Russia, apparently already moving closer to the center in preparation for the next presidential race.

7

The Future of Democratic Consolidation in Russia

The historic events of the 1996 presidential election, especially when considered in conjunction with the 1995 parliamentary elections and the subsequent gubernatorial elections in the fall of 1996, appear to point to real progress in making a Russian democracy. Especially when compared with other periods of Russia's history—be it the confrontational and ultimately bloody politics of the first years of the new Russian state, the seventy years of totalitarian rule under the Communists, or the hundreds of years of autocratic government under the tsars—the following milestones are truly spectacular.

- In December 1995, Russian citizens voted in parliamentary elections. In two rounds of voting in June and July 1996, voters then elected a president. The vote for president was the first time in Russia's thousand-year history that citizens had selected their head of state.

- Despite calls for delay and postponement, these two elections were held on time and under law. These elections were the first to be held under laws drafted and approved through a democratic procedure by elected officials.

- Both of these elections were relatively free and relatively fair. In the presidential election, Yeltsin grossly violated the campaign finance limits, the media openly propagated Yeltsin's cause, and counting irregularities again appeared in Chechnya and some other national republics; but most agreed that these transgressions did not influence the outcome of the vote. Most significantly, all the major actors accepted the election results.

- Large majorities participated in both these elections. In the parliamentary elections, 65 percent of all eligible voters participated, whereas the turnout rates for both rounds of the presidential election approached an amazing 70 percent.

- When given the choice to vote for nationalists, Communists, or the current reform course, Russian voters overwhelmingly rejected the Soviet past and a fascist future and opted to support Boris Yeltsin. By a margin of ten million votes, Boris Yeltsin defeated his communist challenger, Gennadii Zyuganov, in the second round of the presidential election. This electoral result defied the trend in the postcommunist world in which Communists have tended to win second elections.

- After Yeltsin's inauguration, the communist-dominated parliament approved Boris Yeltsin's candidate for prime minister—Viktor Chernomyrdin—by an overwhelming majority. This too was a first, as Russia's elected parliament had never approved the executive's choice for prime minister under the procedures outlined in the legitimate constitution. Later in the year, the Duma passed the government's budget without major political conflict.

- The war in Chechnya has ended, at least temporarily. Although a resolution to the sovereignty issues in question has not been addressed, fighting has stopped. This conclusion of open warfare was the direct result of the presidential electoral process, as both Boris Yeltsin and Alexander Lebed pledged during their campaigns to end the war and then did so after the election.

- Throughout the fall of 1996, dozens of gubernatorial elections were held throughout Russia. Although evidence of falsification has tainted the results in some races, the vast majority were recognized as free and fair by all major participants. Significantly, and against the predictions of most going into the fall electoral season, incumbents supported by Yeltsin's government did not sweep these elections. Rather, the results have been mixed, with independents, Communists, and even a few militant nationalists winning. Aleksandr Rutskoi, the former vice president who led the opposition against Yeltsin in October 1993, was elected governor in Kursk Oblast, and Yevgenii Mikhalov, a leader of Vladimir Zhirinovsky's nationalist Liberal Democratic Party of Russia, won in Pskov Oblast, demonstrating that these elections were not controlled from Moscow.

This series of democratic achievements is remarkable. Yet no one in Russia seems impressed. On the contrary, elites, commentators, and the public have grown noticeably more pessimistic about Russia's future since the conclusion of the presidential election in July 1996.

The magnitude of the wage arrears problem, estimated by Labor Minister Melikyan to be 42 trillion rubles in unpaid wages by the end of 1996, coupled with the government's inability to collect taxes and the lack of economic growth, has fueled speculation of impending social upheaval.[1] Beginning with walkouts by power workers in Primorskii Krai in August 1996, wildcat strikes have increased throughout the country. Discontent within the military also appears to be growing, as the armed forces have not been immune from the government's inability to pay wages. In October 1996, General Boris Gromov, the former commander of the Soviet armed forces in Afghanistan, warned that the armed forces were on the brink of collapse.[2] Two weeks later, Defense Minister Igor Rodionov warned that the "extreme" economic and political instability may produce "unpredictable, catastrophic consequences" for the armed forces and the country as a whole.[3] Prime Minister Chernomyrdin was so worried about unrest in the military that he traveled to Ryazan to reassure paratroopers that their wages were coming. Analysts and politicians alike, including General Alexander Lebed, have speculated that the Russian military was close to a massive mutiny.[4]

Others have predicted renewed tensions between the center and the subjects of the federation. The ten richest regions of Russia have expressed their unwillingness to subsidize the other seventy oblasts, krais, and republics through the inefficient, centralized system of transfer currently in place. Instead, the more outspoken leaders of these donor regions, such as Moscow mayor Yurii Luzhkov, have called for a "new deal" between the federation subjects that would exclude the Russian federal government altogether.[5] Because governors are now elected officials, the prospect of renewed tension between the center and the subjects of the federation seems to be growing.[6]

Public opinion polls suggest that the same electorate that supported Yeltsin overwhelmingly in July does not believe that he or his government can deal with these crises. Yeltsin's approval rating has declined considerably since the 1996 summer ballot. In November, only 10 percent of the Russian population trusted Yeltsin, down from 29 percent in June.[7] More generally, polls conducted by the All-Russian Foundation for Public Opinion (VTsIOM) at the end of 1996 show that people are much less optimistic about the future than they were just months before.[8]

How can we explain this divergence between achievements in the democratization process of the Russian political system and perceptions of the lack of progress? The answer is located in the nature of the Russian state. The Russian rulers that occupy the Russian state have neither the will nor the capacity to meet the demands of their citizens writ large because the state does not represent the interests of society as a whole but rather is deeply penetrated by Russia's emergent capitalist class. In a sense, the state has been privatized by this nouveau riche and thereby operates in the interests of its new owners rather than society as a whole. Consequently, the elections and rituals of a democratic polity more generally have only a temporary influence on the policy process. Once elections are over, the power relations between state and society, which have governed state policy beforehand, return to center stage. Given the tremendous role that big business played in financing Yeltsin's reelection effort, its power actually increased after the 1996 vote.

Interest Intermediation between Russia's State and Society

Since January 1992, when Yeltsin's government initiated radical economic reform, the emergence of a market economy based on private property rights has stimulated the growth of a powerful and new "economic society."[9] Three features of Russia's emerging capitalism are significant to the development of interest articulation within the Russian state. First, capital is concentrated sectorally. Dynamic economic activity is located in trade and services, banking, and the export of raw materials, particularly oil and gas. Production of manufactured goods of any sort has decreased, dramatically in 1990 and 1991 and steadily since. Small enterprise development, after a boom in the late Gorbachev era, has steadily decreased as a percentage share of GNP. Second, capital is concentrated geographically, with an estimated 80 percent of Russia's capital assets located in Moscow. Third, capital is closely tied to the state. Through privatization, the financing of state transfers, and the loans-for-shares program, Russian banks still depend on inside information and money from the state for profits. The intimate relationship between the state and the private sector is even more apparent in sectors exporting raw materials, as the state retains large equity stakes in all these enterprises and a majority share in many and yet refuses to tax them. This relationship between the public and private spheres sustains rent-seeking, not profit-seeking, behavior.

A concentrated, centralized capitalist class—intimately if not parasitically tied to the state—has already left its mark on the preferences of the Russian state. Interest articulation and intermediation are dominated by big business, which crowds out other interest groups lobbying the state.[10] This group's dominance over government leaders and the state was demonstrated most recently during the 1996 presidential election. Although it failed to achieve its first option (the postponement of elections altogether),[11] it decided to abide by the electoral rules and rallied behind one candidate, Boris Yeltsin. Although divided in the past over both political issues and markets, Russia's corporate bosses united during the presidential campaign and provided Yeltsin's campaign with virtually unlimited resources.[12]

In return for this support, this small, well-organized interest group has enjoyed tremendous "representation" within the Russian state since the election, most obviously through appointments. Russia's prime minister, Viktor Chernomyrdin, is the former chairman of Gazprom, Russia's largest company. With Chernomyrdin at the helm, the state has rarely acted against the interests of the oil and gas sector. Russian bankers are also well represented. Their most powerful ally and representative is Anatolii Chubais, who, as the former head of the State Privatization Committee, has been closely tied to Russia's new financiers from the beginning. Allegedly as a condition of their financial support during the campaign, Russia's banking tycoons demanded that Chubais become chief of staff after the election, which he did.[13] Some of these funders of Yeltsin's campaign were not content to have their representatives in government but wanted to try their own hands in the "public" sector. Vladimir Potanin, the former head of the powerful financial group Oneksimbank, became deputy prime minister, and Boris Berezovskii, the head of Logovaz, was given the position of deputy chairman of the Security Council.

As important as these new appointments was the dismissal of the enemies of these plutocrats from Yeltsin's government. As discussed in the previous chapter, Yeltsin fired Deputy Prime Minister Oleg Soskovets, Defense Minister Pavel Grachev, presidential security chief Aleksandr Korzhakov, and Mikhail Barsukov, director of the Federal Security Service (the former KGB) during the presidential campaign. All these political figures were considered enemies of Russia's new business elites and allies of the military-industrial complex. Their departure from the Kremlin and the government created a new balance of power within the state more favorable to the new economic elites.

In March 1997, Yeltsin radically reorganized this first postelection government, strengthening even further the hand of Russia's new capitalist class within the state. Although Vladimir Potanin returned to Oneksimbank, his exit was more than compensated for by the mix of new personnel and portfolios in the top echelons of the government. Most important, Anatolii Chubais moved back to the government to become both first deputy prime minister and finance minister. In essence, he was given complete control of economic policy. Yeltsin also appointed former Nizhny Novogorod governor Boris Nemtsov as first deputy prime minister in charge of social policy, housing reform, and antimonopoly issues. Although not considered a direct representative of Moscow's financial circles, Nemtsov has been firmly identified with the "reformers" during his reign in Nizhny Novogorod. In no way could Nemtsov be considered a enemy of Russia's new capitalist barons. Although less noticed, perhaps the most important cabinet reshuffle concerned the Ministry of Economics. Yeltsin not only appointed a Chubais ally, Mark Urinson, to run this ministry but also approved the subordination of the Industrial Committee and the Committee on Defense Industries to this ministry, a move that effectively eliminated two of the most important government agencies for the military-industrial complex. Additionally, another Chubais protege, Alfred Kokh, was promoted to deputy prime minister while retaining his position as head of the Committee on State Property (GKI). When the dust settled, the cabinet reshuffle signaled a weakening of industrial interests, especially military-industrial interests, and a partial weakening of oil and gas interests, as Chernomyrdin's position was undermined considerably, and a strengthening of the bankers' hand in governmental affairs.

Like other presidential systems, Russia's superpresidentialism privileges big business lobbies and disadvantages mass-based organizations that are better equipped to lobby legislatures than executives.[14] The Duma, however, is not entirely immune to Russia's business lobbies. A well-established system of bribe taking has been formalized within the Duma in which business lobbies pay cash directly to Duma deputies in return for votes. Less audaciously, big business lobbies also have influenced parliamentary factions by financing campaigns in the 1995 elections. In several cases, individual businesspeople bought their positions on a party list. Zhirinovsky's Liberal Democratic Party was most open about offering Duma seats for money, but such transactions also occurred on the Yabloko and Our Home Is Russia lists.

The Weakness of Political Parties

Big business enjoys hegemonic control of the Russian state in part because of the relative weakness of countervailing interest groups and institutions. Most important, Russia's party system remains weak. In pluralist democracies, parties traditionally serve as the principal institutions mediating societal interests within the state. In Russia, however, parties play only a marginal role in interest intermediation. Although elections in Russia have produced positive signs of consolidation since 1993, the legacies of Russia's first failed transition still negatively affect developing a party system in Russia.

As planned, the proportional representation side of Russia's mixed electoral system helped stimulate new party formation in the parliamentary elections in 1993 and again in 1995.[15] Despite these gains, however, Russia's party system remains fragmented and not deeply rooted in either society or the state. Russia still has too many ineffective parties and too few effective parties. In 1993, thirteen parties competed for seats on the PR list; in 1995, forty-three parties made the ballot. The 1995 parliamentary vote may have induced consolidation, as only four of these forty-three parties crossed the 5 percent threshold. Yet all these parliamentary parties have uncertain futures and poor records of representation.

Vladimir Zhirinovsky's Liberal Democratic Party of Russia (LDPR) has created an extensive network of regional offices and local organizers, but it remains unclear whether this organization is a cult movement or a political party, as the organization would collapse almost instantaneously without Zhirinovsky. Our Home Is Russia, the political group founded by Prime Minister Viktor Chernomyrdin, is endowed with significant financial resources, government support, and modest regional organization but easily could follow the fate of earlier "parties of power" in Russia and disintegrate.[16] Grigorii Yavlinsky's Yabloko, the one reformist party not connected to the government that won seats through the proportional system in both 1993 and 1995, most closely resembles a protoparty, complete with a parliamentary faction, grassroots regional organizations, and internal democratic procedures. Yabloko's small faction in the parliament and near lack of penetration of government bodies outside Moscow, however, will assign the nascent party a marginal role in Russian politics in the near future.[17] Only the Communist Party of the Russian Federation (CPRF) looks like a national party, with a well-articulated social base that will outlive its current leaders. Strikingly, however, the Communist Party, the Duma's largest faction, has not demonstrated a proclivity for legislating on behalf of its constituents. Since losing the presidential election in the summer of 1996, the CPRF has grown increasingly cooperative with the government, signaling a rapprochement between old and new political elites that *both* originated from the Communist Party of the Soviet Union.

Outside the Duma, parties play virtually no role at all in aggregating, articulating, or representing societal interests. Yeltsin is an "independent," and his executive administration is insulated from party influence. As in all presidential systems, Russia's strong executive has downgraded the importance of political parties.[18] Likewise, few executive leaders at the oblast, krai, and republic level have open party affiliations. During the cascade of elections of regional executives in the fall of 1996 in which fifty-two leaders were chosen, political parties played only a marginal role in selecting and endorsing candidates.[19] Several newly elected governors, including such prominent partisans as Aleksandr Rutskoi, renounced their party credentials after winning. Most regional legislatures are dominated by local "parties of power" with no ideological affiliation and strong ties to local executive heads.[20]

More generally, the limited number of elected offices and the low frequency of elections to these offices at the subnational level have provided few opportunities for parties to play their organizing function.[21] A nascent party system has emerged in Russia, stimulated primarily by the PR component of the parliamentary electoral system, but this system is still fragmented, centered in Moscow, and thereby peripheral to the organization and articulation of interests in Russia's political system.

The Weakness of Civil Society

The void of mass-based representation left by Russia's weak parties has not been filled. Other economic actors are dwarfed by both the wealth and the political organization of bankers, oil and gas exporters, and their allies. Enterprise directors of former state-owned enterprises, once a relatively unified lobby, have now fractured into several sectoral and regional industrial organizations. Civic Union, the electoral bloc most firmly identified with this economic group, garnered only 1.9 percent of the popular vote in 1993, prompting many factory managers to gravitate back to the "party of power" (Chernomyrdin's bloc and Yeltsin's campaign). Paradoxically, then, enterprise directors throughout a variety of industrial sectors have had a confluence of political interests in the short run with both old money from raw material exporters and new money from Russia's financiers and bankers. Some enterprises of the military-industrial complex have formed alliances with opposition parties and lobbies such the CPRF and Congress of Russian Communities, but the influence of this segment of Russia's economic society has steadily declined since 1992.[22]

Most hurt by the kind of capitalism emerging in Russia have been small businesses and start-up companies. Whereas Poland, a country with a less than a fourth the population of Russia, boasts more than two million private enterprises excluding agriculture, Russia has roughly nine hundred thousand.[23] Exorbitant taxes, inflation, the mafia, and the consolidation of these large financial groups with monopoly control over many markets—in sum, the lack of liberalization—have created an unfriendly environment for the small businessperson. Consequently, this economic interest group, the backbone of many consolidated democracies, is weak, disorganized, and depoliticized in Russia.

Labor is also disoriented and disorganized in the midst of Russia's economic transformation. Old Soviet trade unions, once a tool of control for the Soviet Communist Party, have been slow to meet the new challenges of capitalism. The Federation of Independent Free Trade Unions (FNPR), a consortium of sectorally based unions claiming more than fifty million members, still in most cases identifies with the interests of directors rather than workers. As the interests of management and labor diverge, the FNPR has gradually lost its credibility with both groups, making it politically inconsequential. In the 1996 presidential elections, the FNPR did not endorse a candidate. Nor have independent trade unions filled the void.[24] The Independent Union of Miners, the coalition of strike committees that brought the Soviet government to its knees in 1991, lost its independence and credibility by consistently siding with the Yeltsin government during the past five years. Wildcat strikes, particularly in coal regions and the Far East, persist, giving rise to speculation that Russian labor finally has started to remobilize, but the lack of national organization suggests that these strikes will remain isolated instances.

More generally, participation in overt political activity by civic groups may have peaked in 1990 as part of the nationwide anticommunist movement.[25] Since then, independent civic groups have played less of a role in the organization and conduct of state policy for several reasons: First, the ability of civic groups to articulate and lobby for their interests vis-à-vis the state in Russia's postcommunist era has been impeded by the same factors retarding party development more generally—structural changes in the economy and society, delayed development of pluralist institutions, especially the weakness of representative institutions—and the commensurate ascendancy of executive power. Second, Russia's economic revolution hit hardest against the Soviet-era emergent civil society. As with the labor movement, Russia's new market-embedded society has not sufficiently consolidated to develop market-embedded social organizations. Additionally, postcommunist grassroots organizations have no financial resources, as the "middle class"—the financier of most civic groups in the West—has not emerged yet in Russia. Third, famous anticommunist civic groups such as Memorial (a nationwide grassroots organization dedicated to commemorating the victims of Stalinism) lost their raison d'être in the postcommunist era. The Chechen war briefly mobilized human rights leaders and organizations, but the low level of mass participation in their protests underscored the fact that postcommunist Russian society in January 1995 had developed a new set of concerns and interests different from Soviet society in 1991.[26]

The development of a vibrant postcommunist civil society is further hampered by the sequence and consolidation of Russia's political institutions. The suspension of party development in 1991–1993 served to keep civic groups out of *state* politics. If the party system is underdeveloped, then the ability of civic organizations to influence the state is also impaired. By the time parties began to play a more substantial role in politics (after the 1993 parliamentary elections), the disconnect between political society and civic society was nearly total, as civic organizations saw no benefit from participating in the electoral process and political parties discerned no electoral benefit from catering to allegedly small and ineffective civic groups.[27] Instead of a civil society concerned with influencing the state, Russia has developed an "acivil" society concerned with insulating itself from the state.[28]

Growing executive power at all levels of the Russian state constitutes a final negative influence on Russian state-society relations. Mass-based civic groups are more successful at working with parliaments than with executives. Yeltsin as well as several governors and mayors have created "social chambers," allegedly as a way to compensate for weak representative bodies and to bridge the gap between Russian civic groups and executive power. With few exceptions, however, these advisory councils camouflage, rather than attend to, the growing state-society divide, while undermining the legitimacy of legislative bodies.

This alarming disengagement of society from the state does not mean that a Russian postcommunist civil society has withered away entirely. Civic groups of all stripes still exist, and the number of organizations also continues to grow in postcommunist Russia—a revolutionary improvement over the Soviet era. The danger is rather that civic groups and organizations, however active in their own atomized sphere of work, will involve a smaller and smaller percentage of the population and that civic groups themselves will become increasingly disinterested in and disconnected from the state as a whole, seeking instead to pursue narrow agendas in the private sphere.[29]

The Absence of the Rule of Law

In the evolution of other democracies, well-organized business interests have also assumed disproportionate influence over the state during periods of rapid industrialization or capital accumulation,[30] with mass-based interest groups typically gaining access to the state much later.[31] In the United States, excluded mass-based groups—be they minorities, women, or labor groups— fought for enfranchisement through the independent courts system. This key set of independent institutions does not exist in Russia. The Soviet legacy, of course, has impeded the development of rule of law, as the Soviet communist regime accorded the courts no autonomy whatsoever. Since 1991, the idea of an independent judiciary has been supported in theory by virtually every major political force in Russia, but only a few positive steps have been taken.

Russia's first Constitutional Court relinquished its authority as an arbitrator between the president and parliament in 1993, when the head of the court, Valerii Zorkin, unequivocally sided with White House defenders during the October 1993 crisis. For a year thereafter, the court ceased to function and convened again only after Yeltsin had expanded the number of justices to dilute the voice of his opponents. Since reconvening, the court has made few important decisions.

At lower levels, courts are revamping only slowly to deal with the new challenges of a market economy. Institutionalization of a legal system to protect property rights, govern bankruptcy procedures, enforce contracts, and ensure competition has only just begun. The adoption of the Civil Code (hailed as Russia's "economic constitution") by parliament in 1995 constituted a first step toward creating these institutions but only a first step.[32] In the corporate legal context, laws on disclosure are weak and not enforced, general accounting procedures have not been codified, procedures for shareholder and proxy voting are ambiguous, and institutions governing the payment of dividends do not exist. Consequently, stockholders have little access to information about enterprises in which they have invested. The rule of law has also become weak regarding criminal and civil matters. The combination of a weak state and an incompetent judicial system has produced a sense of anarchy in Russia, a situation alien and frightening to a population accustomed to a powerful authoritarian state. Popular cries for law and order, in turn, threaten to undermine individual liberties and human rights.

State Capacity

The strength of big business, the weakness of political parties, labor, and civil society, and the virtual absence of a rule of law allowed the Russian state to act in the interests of Russia's richest. This configuration not only has impeded democratic consolidation regarding political transformation but also has blocked deepening economic reform. Most important, this small group of financiers and resource exporters has used its dominance over the state to discourage direct foreign investment, its greatest enemy.[33] Perhaps most amazingly, this economic clique has forced the costs of stabilization on Russian laborers. Where else in the world is inflation controlled by simply not paying wages for months at a time! Obviously, the preferences of mass-based interest groups find little voice in Russia's contemporary state configuration.

Even if these mass-based interest groups were articulated, organized, and influential, however, Russia's contemporary state still would
have little capacity to act on their interests. This observation seems
counterintuitive, as the Russian state on paper appears bigger and
more extensive than most states in developed capitalist democracies.
These figures, however, tell little about the state's capacity to *execute*
policy decisions. Neither parliamentary laws nor presidential decrees
are enforced, as the state has little coercive capability against or legitimacy within society. For similar reasons, the state has also been un-
successful at collecting taxes. The state's capacity to act shrinks commensurate to its revenue base. The most respected and capacious state
institutions in Russia are located at the lowest levels of government,
providing another impediment to state action at the federal level.

The consequences of this declining state capacity in Russia have
been dramatic. Basic services traditionally provided by the Soviet/
Russian state such as security, welfare, and education are no longer
public goods.[34] Employees of the state must negotiate and strike just
to be paid for work already completed. At the same time, corruption
within the state remains rampant.

The Russian state, then, has neither the will nor the ability to act
on citizen preferences. To the extent that it functions at all, Russia's
state primarily serves the interests of a small group of business elites
ensconced in Moscow. Pluralist institutions of interest intermediation
are weak; mass-based interest groups are marginal; and the institutions
that could help redress this imbalance—such as a strong parliament
or an independent court system—do not exist. Under these conditions, elections appear ritualistic, bearing little impact on the conduct
or operation of the state. During a brief campaign period, candidates
may seem responsive to popular interests, but once in office a different
set of preferences—the preferences of big business—takes prece-
dence.[35] Under these conditions, it is not be surprising that opinion
polls demonstrate a strong distrust of the government and a lack of
optimism about the future.

Altering the Status Quo

To argue that the state has neither the will nor the capacity to meet the expectations of its citizens does not mean that the situation is unstable or that crisis, breakdown, or revolution is inevitable. On the contrary, weak states dominated by big business and insulated from societal pressures have existed for decades in other countries. Russia may be no different.

Three factors can alter this situation. First, and least likely, leaders currently in control of the state could turn against those that helped bring them to power and begin to attend to the interests of mass-based groups. Yeltsin is the one political actor in the current state who has the capability to carry out a painful and destabilizing reform of the state from within. Thinking about his place in history, Yeltsin perhaps could initiate such a radical reform from within. So far, however, there are few signs that Yeltsin is prepared to initiate such changes, as his health problems have diminished his imprint on the conduct of his government. Nor does his prime minister, Viktor Chernomyrdin, appear intent on initiating new economic reforms. As Anders Aslund concludes regarding those in the Chernomyrdin government, "They are neither for nor against reform but just for the status quo."[36]

Second, an exogenous shock could come from society. For instance, sustained strikes in strategic industries could cripple the current government, as they did the Soviet regime in 1991.[37] Weak states have little capacity to absorb even relatively minor crises. A situation in Primorskii Krai in the fall of 1996 is illustrative. The elected governor of this region, Evgenii Nazdratenko, is considered one of the most authoritarian. He and his government enjoy an intimate relationship with PAKT, a local big business consortium.[38] In the fall of 1996, however, Nazdratenko had to scramble for his political life after workers at the local power station went on strike to demand back wages. Moscow sided with the striking workers and threatened to remove Nazdratenko if he did not pay the wages immediately. Although the governor kept his job in the end, the crisis illustrated that even powerful and elected governors can be quickly undermined by organized mass action.

Third, a presidential election might bring to power new leaders of mass-based groups not beholden to big business and with the will to use the state to serve the interests of a wide segment of the population.[39] Ultimately, the current equilibrium will change only when the state can be deployed to destroy monopolies, tax profit makers, and provide a more favorable environment for market competition. Although a slow process, this change is most likely to happen through the ballot box. Consequently, understanding electoral dynamics in Russia's next presidential vote, whether it is in 1997 or 2000, is critical to any assessment of Russia's democratic future.

The Next Presidential Election

Only months after the July vote, uncertainty surrounding Yeltsin's ability to serve out a second term had launched the next round of presidential positioning, if not outright campaigning. Although the list of candidates poised to compete for the Kremlin remained obvious—Chernomyrdin, Luzhkov, Lebed, Zyuganov, and maybe Boris Nemtsov—the context that will shape a future presidential election has already changed fundamentally.

First, as highlighted above, the path to executive power is much better defined today than it was in July. All serious candidates for Yeltsin's job are making strategic calculations about their futures based on the assumption that the next Kremlin ruler will come to power through the ballot box, not through some other method. All major contenders are either morally committed to the democratic process, strategically optimistic that the easiest way to obtain power is through an election, or too weak to pursue an alternative method.[40] As discussed above, this shared commitment to the electoral process by all major political forces did not exist before the 1996 presidential vote.

Second, the central organizing concept of the 1996 presidential election—communism versus anticommunism—has already disappeared. As discussed in chapter 2, the polarized struggle between two fundamentally different systems shaped every national election from 1990 to 1996. In 1996, this debate ended. The atmosphere of intense polarization and heightened confrontation during the 1996 presidential campaign virtually disappeared after the election. Zyuganov and his party accepted defeat, participated in Yeltsin's inauguration, and then overwhelmingly approved Victor Chernomyrdin as Yeltsin's choice for prime minister. Zyuganov then announced the formation of a new political organization, the National Patriotic Union of Russia (NPSR), which aimed to be more moderate, centrist, and nationalist than the CPRF. Above all else, Zyuganov proclaimed that his new political organization should be understood as a supporter of the current "system" and that he had no revolutionary pretensions to undermine the current regime. The NPSR announced plans to support a dozen candidates in the upcoming cycle of fifty-two gubernatorial elections but specifically avoided backing extremist challengers even if, at times, this moderate policy clashed with the plans of more-radical local Communist Party officials. These gubernatorial elections were virtually devoid of ideology, political platforms, or national issues.[41]

Potential candidates from the so-called party of power, including Prime Minister Viktor Chernomyrdin, Moscow mayor Yurii Luzhkov, or First Deputy Prime Minister Boris Nemtsov, also have realized that the anticommunist card cannot be played again. Chernomyrdin has established regular and intimate contacts with communist leaders. Their coordination on the 1997 budget in December was especially striking. Luzhkov has made performance and concrete achievements—paved roads, new housing, assistance to struggling Moscow enterprises—the trademarks of his political image, not his antipathy to communism. Increasingly, Luzhkov's message has had a patriotic spin, blurring the traditional divisions between reformers and nationalists. Who is the nationalist and who is the liberal when Luzhkov declares that the Ukrainian city of Sevastopol must be returned to Russia and General Lebed actively pursued a peace settlement in Chechnya?

A third difference is that Yeltsin will not be the focal point of the status quo. With Yeltsin's departure, the field of competition between candidates on the reformist ledger will be more level. The fierce rivalries between political leaders and the economic interest groups behind them are unlikely to arrive at a compromise candidate like Boris Yeltsin. Instead, expect brutal competition between presidential hopefuls. Depending on the timing of the next presidential vote, a similar process may unfold within the opposition, especially now that the charismatic Aleksandr Lebed has fallen from grace within the

Yeltsin camp and has the potential to emerge as an opposition leader. The opposition is also more likely to be unified and organized in the next presidential election than are its reformist rivals.

Fourth, as discussed above, Russia does not have interest-based ideological political parties, the kind that shape electoral choices in consolidated democracies. Consequently, Russian citizens will be voting for personalities rather than liberals, conservatives, or social democrats. Big personalities like Lebed and Luzhkov gain from this new context, while gray ones like Chernomyrdin and Zyuganov suffer.

A fifth and final contextual factor has not changed at all: the divide between those benefiting and those suffering from Russia's transition to the market. The thirty million voters who supported Gennadii Zyuganov in July are still solidly opposed to those in power. Although they may not support Zyuganov again, they are unlikely to vote for anyone identified with the status quo such as Chernomyrdin or Yeltsin's chief of staff, Anatolii Chubais. Moreover, we know from previous elections and polling data that these people are most likely to vote, are not easily swayed by national television propaganda, and are worse off today than they were six months ago. Over time, this opposition vote will dissipate, as they are Russia's oldest generation of voters. But in the event of an early election, we expect a substantial part of Russia's electorate to go to an opposition candidate. Today, Lebed is the obvious heir apparent to that large protest vote.

At the same time, the preferences of the forty million that supported Yeltsin in the second round are not as obvious. For many of these voters, fear of communism, not support for the ruling "party of power," motivated their choices in July. With the fear factor fading, these voters will likely split their support among competitors from within the party of power or not vote at all. (Do not expect 70 percent again.) Polls soon after the election showed a sharp decline in popular support for Yeltsin, falling to single digits by December 1996. Moreover, in the new "ideology-free" context, Lebed can compete for these former Yeltsin supporters just as well as Chernomyrdin or Luzhkov. Remember, roughly seven million of Yeltsin's supporters in the second round voted for Lebed in the first.

This new electoral landscape, coupled with the blurring of ideological divisions, gives opposition candidates such as Lebed an immediate advantage and provides less electorally attractive opposition candidates such as Gennadii Zyuganov negotiating leverage with all contenders. If united (a major assumption), the party of power will enjoy unlimited financial support and monopolistic control over national television but will still find it difficult to convince a majority of Russians to vote it into power again.

Its victory, however, is no longer necessary for Russian democracy. With the battle between communism and capitalism over, the greatest threat to either market or democratic development in Russia is no longer Zyuganov or even Lebed but political instability, democratic collapse, or authoritarian rule. That no one seems ready to challenge the existing rules of the game means that the stakes in Russia's next presidential election, no matter who wins, will be much lower than those of the previous election. When understood in this longer time frame, the elections of 1996 may have more far-reaching consequences than were immediately obvious. By helping establish elections as the only the game in town, this precedent-setting milestone may provide the means for democratic renewal in Russia in the future.

Notes

PREFACE

1. For this study, I did not have the financial resources to commission my own polls but was fortunate enough to see most of the major surveys completed by Russian and Western organizations. In the interests of comparability, I have tried to limit most of the citations to polls in this essay to two sources, the Foundation for Public Opinion and the All-Russian Center for the Study of Public Opinion, or VTsIOM. The documents provided by Aleksandr Oslon from the Foundation for Public Opinion contained not only polling data but also statements and analysis about campaign strategy.

INTRODUCTION

1. Peter Reddaway, "Red Alert," *New Republic,* January 29, 1996. For similar interpretations of 1995, see Jerry Hough, Evelyn Davidheiser, and Susan Goodrich Lehman, *The 1996 Russian Presidential Election,* Brookings Occasional Papers (Washington, D.C.: Brookings Institution, 1996), esp. p. 40; Peter Stavrakis, "Russia after the Elections: Democracy or Parliamentary Byzantium?" *Problems of Post-Communism,* March–April 1996, pp. 13–20; Andrei Zhukov, "Yeltsin's Three Blows," *Prism* 2, no. 6 (March 22, 1996): part 2; and Dmitri Glinski, "Yeltsin's Reelection Campaign: A Big Boost to the Communist Cause," *Prism* 2, no. 7 (April 4, 1996): part 3.

2. Quoted in the *Moscow Times,* February 1, 1996.

3. Daniel Singer, "The Burden of Boris," *Nation,* April 1, 1996, p. 23.

4. Hough, Davidheiser, and Lehman, *The 1996 Russian Presidential Election*, p. 86.

5. Liliya Shevtsova, "Yeltsin ostanetsya, dazhe esli proigraet," *Nezavisimaya Gazeta*, April 26, 1996, p. 3.

6. Some have even suggested that voters in postcommunist countries have been rejecting not only first-time leaders but liberal democracy more generally. See Charles Gati, "If Not Democracy, What?" in Michael Mandelbaum, ed., *Post-Communism: Four Perspectives* (New York: Council on Foreign Relations, 1996), pp. 168–98.

7. Marcin Krol, "Poland's Longing for Paternalism," *Journal of Democracy* 5, no. 1 (January 1994): 85–94; Wiktor Osiatynski, "After Walesa: The Causes and Consequences of Walesa's Defeat," *East European Constitutional Review* 4, no. 4 (fall 1995): 35–44.

8. Christine Spolar, "Czech Elections Leave PM, Once Dominant, Position Weakened," *Washington Post*, June 3, 1996, p. A16.

9. Christine Spolar, "Albania Reverts to a One-Party Government," *Washington Post*, June 22, 1996, p. A19.

10. *Transition Report 1995: Investment and Enterprise Development* (London: European Bank for Reconstruction and Development, 1996).

11. As discussed in detail below, Boris Yeltsin controlled all the national television networks and enjoyed an unlimited campaign budget. There was also evidence of falsification in some of Russia's autonomous republics in favor of Boris Yeltsin. Significantly, however, no major presidential candidate challenged the results. For a summary of infractions, see International Republican Institute, *Russia Presidential Observation Report* (Washington, D.C.: International Republican Institute, 1996).

CHAPTER 1

1. O'Donnell and Schmitter have called this electoral phenomenon the *pendular effect* in transitions. See Guillermo O'Donnell and Philippe Schmitter, *Transitions from Authoritarian Rule: Tentative Conclusions about Uncertain Democracies* (Baltimore, Md.: Johns Hopkins University Press, 1986), p. 62.

2. Adam Przeworski, *Democracy and the Market: Political and Economic Reforms in Eastern Europe and Latin America* (Cambridge: Cambridge University Press, 1991); and Claus Offe, "Capitalism by Democratic Design? Democratic Theory Facing the Triple Transition in East Central Europe," *Social Research* 58 (winter 1991).

3. Marcin Krol, "Poland's Longing for Paternalism," *Journal of Democ-*

racy 5, no. 1 (January 1994): 85–94; Osiatynski, "After Walesa," pp. 35–44.

4. Morris Fiorina, *Retrospective Voting in American National Elections* (New Haven: Yale University Press, 1981).

5. O'Donnell and Schmitter, *Transitions from Authoritarian Rule*, p. 62.

6. This learning period takes longer in postcommunist transitions, as the traditional class-based identities in society are also in flux. On the debatable relationship between social structure and party development in the postcommunist world, see Herbert Kitschelt, "The Formation of Party Systems in East Central Europe," *Politics and Society* 20, no.1 (1992): 7–50; Valerie Bunce and Maria Csanadi, "Uncertainty in the Transition: Postcommunism in Hungary," *East European Politics and Society* 7 (1993): 240–75; Geoffrey Evans and Stephen Whitefield, "Identifying the Bases of Party Competition in Eastern Europe," *British Journal of Political Science* 23, no. 4 (1993): 521–48; and M. Steven Fish, "The Advent of Multipartism in Russia, 1993–1995," *Post-Soviet Affairs* 11, no. 4 (October–December 1995), pp. 340–83.

7. For summaries and discussions of all these elections, see Michael McFaul and Nikolai Petrov, eds., *Politicheskii Al'manakh Rossii 1995* (Moscow: Moscow Carnegie Center, 1997). For a comprehensive discussion of all national elections, see Stephen White, Richard Rose, and Ian McAllister, *How Russia Votes* (London: Chatham House, 1997).

8. Russell Bova, "Political Dynamics of the Post-Communist Transition: A Comparative Perspective," in Nancy Bermeo, ed., *Liberalization and Democratization: Change in the Soviet Union and Eastern Europe* (Baltimore, Md.: Johns Hopkins University Press, 1992), pp. 113–38; Philippe Schmitter with Terry Karl, "The Conceptual Travels of Transitologists and Consolidologists: How Far to the East Should They Attempt to Go?" *Slavic Review* 53, no. 1 (spring 1994): 173–85; and Valerie Bunce, "Should Transitologists Be Grounded?" *Slavic Review* 54, no. 1 (spring 1995): pp. 111–27.

9. For an explication of this approach to the study of Russian politics, see Michael McFaul, "Revolutionary Transformations in Comparative Perspective: Defining a Post-Communist Research Agenda," in David Holloway and Norman Naimark, eds., *Reexamining the Soviet Experience: Essays in Honor of Alexander Dallin* (Boulder, Colo.: Westview Press, 1996); McFaul, "Prospects for Democratic Consolidation in Russia," in Larry Diamond and Marc Plattner, eds., *Consolidating the Third Wave Democracies* (Baltimore, Md.: Johns Hopkins University Press, 1997); and McFaul, "Party Formation after Revolutionary Transitions: The Russian Case," in

Alexander Dallin, ed., *Political Parties in Russia* (Berkeley, Calif.: International and Area Studies, 1993), pp. 7–28. A similar approach is developed in Walter Conner, *Tattered Banners: Labor, Conflict, and Corporatism in Postcommunist Russia* (Boulder, Colo.: Westview Press, 1996).

10. O'Donnell and Schmitter, *Transitions from Authoritarian Rule*, p. 69.

11. Zygmunt Bauman, "A Revolution in the Theory of Revolutions?" *International Political Science Review* 15, no. 1 (1994): 15–24.

12. The Russia case includes a third component: transforming an empire into a region of independent sovereign states. On this triple transition, see McFaul, "Prospects for Democratic Consolidation in Russia."

13. M. Steven Fish, *Democracy from Scratch: Opposition and Regime in the New Russian Revolution* (Princeton, N.J.: Princeton University Press, 1996).

14. Rivera, "Historical Cleavage or Transition Mode?"; and Evans and Whitefield, "Identifying the Bases of Party Competition in Eastern Europe." In correctly identifying the impeding effects of socioeconomic reorganization for party development, Evans and Whitefield then wrongly predict high volatility in voter preferences because they do not take into account the organizing and stabilizing effects of this cleavage concerning voter attitudes toward the revolution.

15. Of course, there was variation within the postcommunist world regarding the degree of interest formation and articulation at the start of transition. In Poland, for example, peasant ownership of land during communist rule meant that this class or group already had well-defined interests from the very beginning of transition.

16. See Geoffrey Pridham and Paul Lewis, eds., *Stabilising Fragile Democracies: Comparing New Party Systems in Southern and Eastern Europe* (London: Routledge, 1996).

17. On modes of transition, see Terry Karl and Philippe Schmitter, "Democratization around the Globe: Opportunities and Risks," in Michael Klare and Daniel Thomas, eds., *World Security: Challenges for a New Century* (New York: St. Martin's Press, 1994), pp. 43–62; and Terry Karl, "Dilemmas of Democratization in Latin America," *Comparative Politics* 23, no. 1 (October 1990): 1–21.

18. On the importance of pacts for successful transitions, see O'Donnell and Schmitter, *Transitions from Authoritarian Rule;* and Juan Linz and Alfred Stepan, *Problems of Democratic Transition and Consolidation: Southern Europe, South America, and Post-Communist Europe* (Baltimore, Md.: Johns Hopkins University Press, 1996), chap. 3. These authors do not argue that pacts are necessary for a successful transitions to democracy but

rather that pacted transitions are more likely to succeed than nonpacted transitions.

19. Following from Dankwart Rustow, many writers on democratic transitions assume that compromise is both the only and the preferred solution to a stalemated situation. Although perhaps preferred, revolutionary transitions demonstrate that compromise is not the only possible outcome to stalemate. Rather, options with different payoffs (both higher and lower) are also available. On the "virtues of deadlock" in the Russia case, see Steven Fish, "Russia's Crisis and the Crisis of Russology," in Holloway and Naimark, *Reexamining the Soviet Experience,* pp. 158–61. Rustow's seminal article is "Transitions to Democracy: Toward a Dynamic Model," *Comparative Politics* 2, no. 3 (April 1970): 337–63.

20. Aleksandr Shabanov, deputy chairman of the KPRF, speech at the Moscow Carnegie Center, March 28, 1996.

21. The model of revolutionary transition sketched here, in which a central characteristic of a revolutionary situation is multiple sovereignty, draws from Samuel Huntington, *Political Order and Changing Societies* (New Haven, Conn: Yale University Press, 1968), chap. 5; Charles Tilly, *From Mobilization to Revolution* (New York: McGraw-Hill, 1976), chap. 9; Peter Amman, "Revolution: A Redefinition," *Political Science Quarterly* 77, no. 1 (March 1962); and Leon Trotsky, *The History of the Russian Revolution* (New York: Simon and Shuster, 1932).

22. Author's interview with Aleksandr Oslon, president of the Foundation of Public Opinion and chief pollster for the Yeltsin campaign in 1996 (December 13, 1996). See also William Zimmerman, "Foreign Policy, Political System Preference, and the Russian Presidential Election of 1996," paper presented to the American Association for the Advancement of Slavic Studies, Boston, November 16, 1996.

23. On the differences between the "personal experiences" hypothesis and the "national assessments" hypothesis, see Roderick Kiewiet, *Macroeconomics and Micro-politics: The Electoral Effects of Economic Issues* (Chicago: University of Chicago Press, 1983), pp. 15–20.

24. For arguments that treat voters as prospective, concerned more with the national economy than personal economic circumstances, see Michael MacKuen, Robert Erikson, and James Stimson, "Peasants or Bankers? The American Electorate and the U.S. Economy," *American Political Science Review* 86, no. 3 (September 1992): 597–611; Kiewet, *Macro-economics and Micro-politics*; and Donald Kinder and Roderick Kiewiet, "Sociotropic Politics: The American Case," *British Journal of Political Science* 11 (1981): 129–62.

25. Fiorina, *Retrospective Voting in American National Elections;* V.O. Key, *The Responsible Electorate* (New York: Vintage, 1966); and Anthony Downs, *An Economic Theory of Democracy* (New York: Harper and Row, 1957).

26. Fiorina, *Retrospective Voting in American National Elections,* p. 15.

27. For an argument that highlights the importance of pork-barrel politics, see Dan Triesman, "Why Yeltsin Won," *Foreign Affairs,* fall 1996.

28. On the business-cycle theory, see Eduard Tufte, *Political Control of the Economy* (Princeton, N.J.: Princeton University Press, 1978).

29. Key, *Responsible Electorate,* p. 61.

30. Samuel Popkin makes a similar claim regarding recent American presidential elections in *The Reasoning Voter: Communication and Persuasion in Presidential Campaigns* (Chicago, Ill.: University of Chicago Press, 1994).

31. Moreover, the literature on U.S. elections suggests that a generation must pass before party identification plays a salient role, as the party label is usually passed through families. See part three of Warren Miller and Merrill Shanks, *The New American Voter* (Cambridge, Mass.: Harvard University Press, 1996).

32. Here, I am reporting the results of the first question, which asked, "Do you trust Russian president Yeltsin?" Yeltsin also won the second question, which asked, "Do you approve of the socioeconomic policy conducted by the Russian president and by the Russian government since 1992?" To this question, 53 percent answered yes.

33. On this debate, see Michael McFaul, "Russia between Elections: The Vanishing Center," *Journal of Democracy* 7, no. 2 (April 1996): 90–104; and Mikhail Myagkov, Peter Ordeshook, and Alexander Sobyanin, "The Russian Electorate from 1991 to 1995," ms., Caltech, May 14, 1996.

34. On this divide, see Ralph Clem and Peter Craumer, "The Politics of Russia's Regions: A Geographic Analysis of the Russian Election and Constitutional Plebiscite of December 1993," *Post-Soviet Geography* 36, no. 2 (1994): 67–87; Nikolai Petrov, "Elektoralnyi landshaft Rossii i ego evolutsiya," in Michael McFaul and Nikolai Petrov, eds., *Politicheskii Almanakh Rossii 1995* (Moscow: Moscow Carnegie Center, 1995), pp. 28–44; Darrell Slider, Vladimir Gimpelson and Sergei Chugrov, "Political Tendencies in Russia's Regions: Evidence from the 1993 Parliamentary Elections," *Slavic Review* 53, no. 3 (fall 1994): 711–32; and Robert Orttung and Scott Parrish, "Duma Votes Reflect North-South Divide," *Transition* 2, no. 4 (February 26, 1996): 12–14.

35. For this breakdown of the 1995 elections, see Nikolai Petrov, "Analyz resultatov vyborov 1995 g. v Gosudarstvennuyu umu RF po okrugam

i regionam," ms., Moscow Carnegie Center, February 1996, table 10. See also "Politicheskie nastroeniya regional'noi administrativnoi elity Rossii" (a document prepared by Leonid Smirnyagin of the Analytical Center of the Russian Presidential Administration and leaked to the press), *Nezavisimaya Gazeta*, February 11, 1996.

36. For evidence on this correlation from the 1995 elections, see Igor Klyamkin, "Politicheskie predpochteniya pazlichnykh sotsial'no-professional'nikh grupp rossiiskogo obshchestva na parlamenskikh vyborakh 1995 goda," ms., Moscow Carnegie Center, February 1996, p. 3. Curiously, the urban-rural and generational divides just described also formed the battle lines for Russia's first revolution in 1917. The so-called red belt areas that has supported the communist candidates recently was the area that most vehemently resisted the Bolsheviks in 1917. The correlation between age and support for the market revolution in the 1990s mirrors the same correlation between age and bolshevism earlier in the century.

37. See John Earle and Richard Rose, "Ownership Transformation, Economic Behavior, and Political Attitudes in Russia," working paper, Stanford, Calif., Center for International Security and Arms Control, August 1996.

CHAPTER 2

1. Juan Linz, "Presidential or Parliamentary Democracy: Does It Make a Difference?" and Arend Lijphart, "Presidentialism and Majoritarian Democracy," in Juan Linz and Arturo Valenzuela, eds., *The Failure of Presidential Democracy: Comparative Perspectives*, vol. 1 (Baltimore, Md.: Johns Hopkins University Press, 1994).

2. For explication, see Thomas Remington and Steven Smith, "Political Goals, Institutional Context, and the Choice of an Electoral System: The Russian Parliamentary Election Law," *American Journal of Political Science* 40, no. 4 (November 1996): 1253–79.

3. This tendency is often called Duverger's law or Duverger's rule. See Maurice Duverger, *Political Parties: Their Organization and Activity in the Modern State* (New York: Wiley, 1954).

4. See Linz, "Presidential or Parliamentary Democracy"; Matthew Shugart and John Carey, *Presidents and Assemblies* (Cambridge: Cambridge University Press, 1992), chap. 2; and Giovanni Sartori, *Comparative Constitutional Engineering* (New York: New York University Press, 1994), chap. 5.

5. Theoretically, the district magnitude could be greater than one, as

a collective executive might be possible. See Shugart and Carey, *Presidents and Assemblies.*

6. Liphart, "Presidentialism and Majoritarian Democracy," esp. pp. 97–99.

7. Linz, "Presidential or Parliamentary Democracy," p. 19.

8. Shugart and Carey, *Presidents and Assemblies*, chap. 8.

9. The financial rules of the campaign further encouraged these candidates, as presidential hopefuls who pulled out before the first round were required to pay for the free television and radio time they had received as presidential candidates.

10. This is how Alberto Fujimori emerged from nowhere to be elected president in Peru. The same pattern was repeated in Belarus, when the relatively unknown Aleksandr Luakshenko won in a majority run-off system. On Fujimori, see Gregory Schmidt, "Fujimori's 1990 Upset Victory in Peru," *Comparative Politics* 28 (April 1996): 321–54; and Shugart and Carey, *Presidents and Assemblies*, pp. 214–15.

11. Elena Trgybova, "Vybory prezidenta naznacheny 'orientirovochno' na 16 yunya 1996 goda," *Segodnya*, May 5, 1995, p. 1.

12. Shugart and Carey, *Presidents and Assemblies*, chap. 9.

13. In the one election in which voters cast separate ballots in a binary "presidential" way (the referendum on the constitution) and in a multiparty election (the parliamentary elections), the results varied. Although more than 50 percent of participating voters ratified the president's constitution in the referendum, only 33 percent of these same voters supported proreformist political parties on the multiparty ballot.

14. Institutionally, presidential systems in general encourage weak parties and fragmented party systems. See Lijphart, "Presidentialism and Majoritarian Democracy," p. 98.

15. Author's interview with presidential adviser Giorgii Satarov, November 1995. According to some Kremlin officials, Yeltsin pressured Chernomyrdin to form a new bloc and run in the parliamentary elections as an act of self-destruction. Strikingly, Yeltsin never endorsed the bloc during the parliamentary campaign or associated with Our Home during his presidential bid. Officials in the Congress of Russian Communities (KRO) tell a similar story about presidential manipulation regarding General Lebed. Although obviously the most popular and charismatic leader with KRO, Lebed was not allowed to campaign freely or appear in major roles in KRO television advertisements. Instead, Yurii Skokov, Yeltsin's former head of the Security Council, dominated the campaign and overshad-

owed Lebed, resulting in a disappointing electoral result for KRO. Several KRO officials were convinced that Skokov was sent by the Kremlin to deliberately sabotage Lebed and the bloc's electoral prospects.

16. Shakkum won 277,068 votes; Bryntsalov, 123,065.

17. Lee Hockstader and David Hoffman, "Yeltsin Campaign Rose from Tears to Triumph," *Washington Post,* July 7, 1996, p. A1.

18. Aleksandr Mekhanik, "Prezidentskie vybory i stanovlenie politi-cheskoi sistemy v Rossii," *Segodnya,* June 6, 1996, p. 5.

19. Michael McFaul, *Russia between Elections: What the 1995 Parliamentary Elections Really Mean* (Washington, D.C.: Carnegie Endowment for International Peace, 1996).

CHAPTER 3

1. See Michael McFaul, *Understanding Russia's 1993 Parliamentary Elections: Implications for U.S. Foreign Policy* (Stanford: Hoover Institution Press, 1994).

2. Vladimir Lysenko, "Avtoritarnyi Rezhim Neizbezhen," *Nezavisimaya Gazeta,* December 22, 1994; Yegor Gaidar, speech before party activists, December 19, 1994.

3. Vladimir Bokser at a seminar sponsored by the National Democratic Institute on the December 1993 elections, December 8, 1994; and Aleksandr Tsipko at a seminar sponsored by the Carnegie Center in Moscow, January 26, 1995.

4. In December 1994, Yeltsin's security guards harassed Vladimir Gusinskii, the head of Most Bank, in a standoff in downtown Moscow. Kremlin security forces beat Gusinskii's personal guards, holding some of them at gunpoint for several hours. At the time, Gusinskii's television network, NTV, ran coverage critical of Yeltsin. By 1996, however, Gusinskii and NTV had endorsed Yeltsin and worked vigorously to aid his reelection effort.

5. Author's interview with Vladimir Bokser, one of the founders and leaders of Democratic Russia, April 1994.

6. Yeltsin's hostility to party development is typical of elected executives in democratic transitions. See Guillermo O'Donnell, "Delegative Democracy," *Journal of Democracy* 5, no. 1 (January 1994): 55–69; and Linz, "Presidential or Parliamentary Democracy," pp. 27–28.

7. Author's interviews with former aides to Prime Minister Gaidar, June 1994.

8. Emil' Pain and Arkadii Popov, "Vlast' i obshchestvo na barrika-dakh," *Izvestiya*, February 10, 1995, p. 4.

9. On this group, see John Dunlop, "The 'Party of War' and Russian Imperial Nationalism," *Problems of Post-Communism*, March/April 1996, pp. 29–34.

10. Author's conversations with Korzhakov's deputies, March 1996.

11. Yeltsin named First Deputy Prime Minister Oleg Soskovets his campaign manager. Known as a hard-liner with close ties to the military-industrial complex, Soskovets has virtually no campaign experience. Moreover, his appointment effectively marginalized liberals within the Kremlin within the campaign, including, most important, Georgii Satarov.

12. Yeltsin also appointed a new head of the State Property Committee (GKI), Aleksandr Kazakov, a former member of the presidential apparatus thought to be more conservative than either Chubais, the first head of the GKI, or the outgoing Sergei Belayev.

13. Quoted in Michael Specter, "Grim Yeltsin Blames Own Government for Russia's Ills," *New York Times*, February 24, 1996, p. 3.

14. Valerii Vyzhutovich, "Staraya Ploshchad, novaya komanda," *Izvestiya*, March 26, 1996, p. 1.

15. Soskovets hired three U.S. campaign consultants to assist his electoral team, but they arrived in Moscow at roughly the same time that he was pushed aside. With the possible exception of Yeltsin's daughter, no one from the Chubais campaign team met with (let alone received advice from) these advisers. For accounts, see Michael Kramer, "Yanks to the Rescue," *Time* 148, no. 4 (July 15, 1996): 28–32; and Michael McFaul, "Yanks Brag, Press Bites," *Weekly Standard* 1, no. 43 (July 22, 1996): 14–15.

16. Author's interview with presidential adviser Georgii Satarov, March 26, 1996.

17. Fortunately for Yeltsin, several groups emerged spontaneously to collect signatures to register his candidacy. A group organized by Vladimir Komchatov, presidential representative to Moscow, and Lev Shamaev, from the Foundation for the Support of the First President, eventually delivered the necessary signatures to register Yeltsin as a candidate.

18. The strategy's imminent failure was apparent to outsiders as well. Speaking in February, Anders Aslund incisively stated, "I can't see any possibility whatsoever that President Yeltsin will even reach the second round of the presidential election. What he's doing now is pursuing a

policy that alienates all his previous supporters. The Nationalists and the Communists hate him anyhow, so I can't see who outside of the narrow power structure that would vote for him. His policy makes no sense." (Aslund, commenting on the *Newshour with Jim Lehrer*, February 14, 1996, transcript, p. 3.)

19. Author's interview with Aleksei Kara-Muza, one of the participants in these drafting sessions, July 7, 1996.

20. Chrystia Freeland, John Thornhill, and Andrew Gowers, "Moscow's Group of Seven," *Financial Times*, November 1, 1996, p. 15.

21. See David Remnick, "The War for the Kremlin," *New Yorker*, July 22, 1996. On these financiers, see the excellent survey by Betsy McKay, "Russia's Guilded Age," *Central European Economic Review*, June 1996.

22. Author's interview with Vyacheslav Nikonov, deputy chairman of ODOP and Yeltsin campaign press secretary, September 18, 1996.

23. "Shtabnye ucheniya v Kremle," *Rossiiskaya Gazeta*, March 26, 1996, p. 1. Later, Eduard Sagalaev, head of RTR network (channel two), and Anatolii Chubais also joined this council. See Aleksei Mukhin, Andrei Zapeklyi, and Nikita Tyukov, *Rossiya: Presidenskaya Kampaniya—1996* (Moskva: SPIK-Tsentr, 1996), p. 13.

24. Author's interviews with Satarov, March 26, 1996, Nikonov, September 18, 1996, and a member of the Oleg Soskovets campaign team, September 17, 1996, who asked not be identified. Soon after this reorganization, several of the campaign specialists working for Soskovets moved on to run Aleksandr Yakovlev's mayoral campaign in Saint Petersburg. Eventually that election pitted one candidate, Anatolii Sobchak, backed by Ilyushin and Chubais, against another, Yakovlev, backed by Soskovets and Korzhakov. Yakovlev won.

25. Cited in Alessandra Stanley, "With Campaign Staff in Disarray, Yeltsin Depends on Perks of Office," *New York Times*, May 13, 1996, p. 5.

26. Author's interview with Igor Kharichev, aide to Filatov, March 30, 1996.

27. Author's interview Nikonov, September 18, 1996.

28. "Spisok obshchestvennikh ob'denennii, uchastovavshikh v uchreditel'noi konferentsii po sozdaniyu dvizheniya v podderzhku B.N. Yeltsina," mimeo, March 1996.

29. Author's interview with Vladimir Lepekhin, one of the people originally hired on this team, June 30, 1996.

30. See the interview with Sergei Lisovskii, general director of ORT-Advertising and author of this campaign in *Nezavisimaya Gazeta*, June 8,

1996, p. 6. On the cost, see Elena Dikun and Lev Sigal, "Milliardy dlya diktatury elektorata," *Obshchaya Gazeta,* June 20–26, 1996, p. 8.

31. See Peter Rutland, "Yeltsin's Future Hangs in the Balance as Elections Loom," *OMRI Analytical Brief* 1, no. 103 (May 10, 1996): 1.

32. Bunin, presentation at the Moscow Carnegie Center, March 30, 1996.

33. Quoted here in *OMRI Russian Presidential Election Survey*, no. 5 (May 29, 1996).

34. Aleksei Titkov, "Kampaniya v regionakh i ee effektivnost'," *Presidentskie vybory v Rossii,* no. 9 (Moscow) (June 1996).

35. Fond "Obshchestvennoe mnenie," "Klyuchevye problemy predvybornoi kampanii v zerkale obshchestvennogo mneniya," *Rezultaty sotsiologicheskikh issledovannii,* no. 29 (May 10, 1996): 2. I am indebted to Aleksandr Oslon, president of the Foundation for Public Opinion and chief pollster for the Yeltsin camapaign, for providing me access to these internal campaign documents.

36. Ibid., p. 4.

37. Author's interview with Aleksandr Olson, chief pollster for the Yeltsin campaign, and president of the Foundation for Public Opinion, December 13, 1996. In exit polls conducted by Mitovsky International and CESSI during first-round voting in June, the three most important issues identified were back wages and pensions (35%), the economy (25%), and Chechnya (20%). Crime was identified by only 13 percent of Russian voters as the most important issue while a meager 2 percent cited foreign policy. See the *New York Times,* June 18, 1996, p. A4.

38. See the remarks by Yeltsin's aide Vyacheslav Volkov in *Monitor—a Daily Briefing on the Post-Soviet States* 2, no. 103 (May 24, 1996): 5.

39. In fact, most of the estimated 31 million rubles in unpaid wages at the time were owed to workers by private enterprises, not the state. The public perception of the problem, however, was that the federal government was at fault.

40. "Vremya," ORT, March 27, 1996.

41. "Den'gi budut v nachale aprelya," *Krasnaya Zvezda,* March 23, 1996, p. 1; "Plan vypolnen," *Nezavisimaya Gazeta,* March 30, 1996, p. 1.

42. Fond "Obshchestvennoe mnenie," "Klyuchevye problemy predvybornoi kampanii v zerkale obshchestvennogo mneniya," *Rezultaty sotsiologicheskikh issledovannii,* no. 29 (May 10, 1996): 4–5.

43. "Luchshaya operatsiya chechenskoi voiny," *Moskovokskii Komsomolets,* May 29, 1996, p. 1.

44. Obrashchenie chetvertogo s'ezda partii, "Demokraticheskii Vybor Rossii" k grazhdam' rossii," *Demokraticheskii Vybor* 1, no. 1 (May 18, 1996): 1.

45. Author's interview with DVR Executive Committee member Mikhail Schneider, July 6, 1996. After the DVR decision to back Yeltsin, Schneider joined the campaign and worked directly for Satarov.

46. Through a tremendous effort that relied almost exclusively on volunteers, Lebed's team of retired military officers managed to collect the million signatures needed to register their candidate. The campaign, however, had wasted all its resources on the signature drive and was totally broke before the campaign began. The details of Lebed's campaign follow.

47. According to the author's interviews with Dmitrii Rogozin, head of the Congress of Russian Communities; an assistant to Korzhakov; and members of Yeltsin's campaign team (conducted in July and September 1996), Lebed first initiated contacts with Korzhakov through Rogozin in late March. After a couple of meetings with Korzhakov (meetings closely monitored by Chubais and Satarov), the terms of the agreement were then presented to Yeltsin. Initially, Lebed was to be offered the post of minister of defense. After his strong showing in the first round, however, his demands increased.

48. For details, see the section on Lebed below.

49. Fond "Obshchestvennoe mnenie," "Vozmozhnye 'peretekaniya' golosov mezhdu elektoratami politicheskikh liderov," *Rezultaty sotsiologicheskikh issledovannii*, no. 10 (April 22, 1996): 1–2.

50. Author's interviews with Boris Saltikovskii, Yeltsin campaign strategist, June 24, 1996; Yuliya Rusova, campaign manager for Lebed, June 26, 1996; and Dmitrii Rogozin, KRO leader and adviser to Lebed, September 18, 1996.

51. This assumption proved to be true, as VTsIOM's exit poll showed that 64 percent of Yavlinsky's supporters in the first round voted for Yeltsin in the second round. (VTsIOM, "Ekspress 96–20," mimeo, July 12, 1996, p. 2.)

52. See the remarks by Anatolii Chubais speaking to the Democratic Choice of Russia conference, April 27, 1996, as quoted in *OMRI Russian Presidential Election Survey*, no. 1 (May 3, 1996): 5.

53. Mukhin, Zapeklyi and Tyukov, *Rossiya: Presidenskaya Kampaniya— 1996*, p. 31. Other examples were reported to the author by Yabloko campaign activists.

54. "Yeltsin Offered Rival a Market Reform Post," *New York Times*, May 19, 1996, p. 6.

55. Yavlinsky's list of demands to Yeltsin was published in *Izvestiya*, May 18, 1996, p. 2. See also Giorgii Bovt and Natal'ya Kalashnikova, "Peshka trebuet pozhertvovat' ferzya," *Kommsersant'-Daily*, May 18, 1996, p. 3.

56. Quoted here from Michael Specter, "Bid for Coalition to Bar Communist Fades in Moscow," *New York Times*, May 18, 1996, p. 1.

57. Ibid., p. 4.

58. All these polls can be found on the World Wide Web at "http://www.cs.indiana.edu/hyplan/dmiguse/Russia/polls.html."

59. Author's interview with Vyacheslav Nikonov, Yeltsin's campaign spokesperson and deputy chairman of ODOP, September 18, 1996.

60. Vladimir Bokser, Vasilii Ostashev, and Michael McFaul, "Ne puti komumnistov—boloto," ms., Moscow Carnegie Center, May 1996.

61. Vladimir Zharikin, "Prezidenta vyberut tsentristy," *Rossiiskaya Gazeta*, March 21, 1996.

62. This composite snapshot of the Russian centrist voter is the description provided to the author during interviews with several officials in the Yeltsin campaign. It is based on survey research conducted by the Foundation for Public Opinion and focus group work conducted by the Center for Political Technologies.

63. Presentation by Leonid Sedov, deputy director of the All-Russian Center for the Study of Public Opinion (VTsIOM), at the Carnegie Moscow Center, March 30, 1996.

64. Fond "Obshchestvennoe mnenie," "Klyuchevye problemy predvybornoi kampanii v zerkale obshchestvennogo mneniya," *Rezultaty sotsiologicheskikh issledovannii*, no. 29 (May 10, 1996): 2.

65. Yeltsin speech in Kazan', as reported on Itogi, June 9, 1996.

66. Quoted in *OMRI Daily Digest*, no. 97 (May 20, 1996): part 1.

67. "Gradonachal'niki kabinetov ne menyayut," *Rossiiskaya Gazeta*, March 26, 1996, p. 2. This newspaper is controlled by the government.

68. Yeltsin speaking in Saint Petersburg, June 14, 1996, as quoted on ORT, June 14, 1996.

69. See Mukhin, Zapeklyi, and Tyukov, *Rossiya: Presidenskaya Kampaniya*, pp. 27–28.

70. Boris Vinogradov, "'Soyuz chetyrikh—vser'ez i hadolgo, po men'shei mere—na 5 let," *Izvestiya*, March 30, 1996, p. 1.

71. Patrick Henry, "Russia, Belarus Sign Sweeping Union Pact," *Moscow Times*, April 3, 1996, p. 1.

72. Quoted in *OMRI Russian Presidential Election Survey*, no. 5 (May 29, 1996).

73. *OMRI Daily Digest*, no. 97 (May 20, 1996): part 1.

74. "Backing Boris: Summiteering, Electioneering, and Debt Relief," *Prism: A Bi-Weekly on the Post-Soviet States* 11, no. 9 (May 3, 1996): part 1.

75. See especially his campaign platform, "Bydem vmeste!" *Rossiiskaya Gazeta*, July 1–7, 1996, p. 2.

76. Quoted in Alessandra Stanley, "With Campaign Staff in Disarray, Yeltsin Depends on Perks of Office," *New York Times*, May 13, 1996, p. 1.

77. "Novoe svidetel'stvo obostreniya predvybornoi bor'by," *Nezavisimaya Gazeta*, June 8, 1996, p 1; and interview with Yeltsin, *Itogi*, NTV, June 9, 1996.

78. According to senior Yeltsin campaign organizers (who asked not to be identified), these responses were planned and scripted in Moscow well before the vote. (Author's interviews, March 28, 1996.)

79. A full list, description, and discussion of these decrees can be found in Mukhin, Zapeklyi, and Tyukov, *Rossiya: Presidenskaya Kampaniya*, pp. 35–38.

80. Yeltsin, as quoted on Interfax, ORT, and Russian TV, Vremya, May 23, 1996.

81. *Monitor—a Daily Briefing on the Post-Soviet States* 2, no. 103 (May 24, 1996).

82. *OMRI Daily Digest*, no. 105 (May 30, 1996): part 1.

83. Tat'yana Malkina, "Boris Yeltsin zamakhnulsya na kvartirnyi vopros," *Segodnya*, March 30, 1996, p. 1.

84. Richard Boudreaux, "Stumping Yeltsin Tries On Guise of 'Good Tsar,'" *Los Angeles Times*, May 13, 1996, p. A10.

85. *OMRI Daily Digest*, no. 103 (May 28, 1996): part 1.

86. Ibid.

87. Treisman, "Why Yeltsin Won."

88. According to an analysis conducted by the Yeltsin campaign team and confirmed by Nikolai Petrov and Aleksei Titkov from the Moscow Carnegie Center, regions in which Yeltsin pledged financial support did not vote in greater numbers for Yeltsin than would have been predicted from 1995 parliamentary results in which state largesse was not a factor.

See Nikolai Petrov and Aleksei Titkov, "Politicheskaya Geographiya Rossii: Novaya ili Staraya?" in *Prezidenskie vybory v Rossii*, no. 9 (June 1996).

89. Author's interview with Nikonov. In this interview, Nikonov told the story of local reactions to a Yeltsin decision to give away a tractor to a farmer in Krasnodar. Although the individual farmer and his family were quite pleased with the president and stated that they planned to vote for him, Yeltsin's rating in the region as a whole went down, as others polled there resented the fact that they were not the direct beneficiaries of Yeltsin's generosity.

90. For an excellent account of this support, see Aleksei Zudin, "Biznes i politika v prezidentskoi kampanii 1996 goda, *Pro et Contra* 1, no. 1 (October 1996): 46–60.

91. *OMRI Russian Presidential Election Survey*, no. 3 (May 16, 1996).

92. Aleksandr Bekker, "Zapad idet na vyruchku rossiiskim vlastyam," *Segodnya*, March 28, 1996, p. 1.

93. Official campaign expenditures for all candidates can be found in *Vestnik Tsentral'noi Komissii Rossiiskoi Federatsii* 32, no. 12 (1996): 92–103.

94. European Institute for the Media, "Media and the Russian Presidential Elections," *Newsletter*, no. 2 (June 4, 1996).

95. Sophia Coudenhove, "Russian Papers Press Hard for Yeltsin," *Moscow Times*, June 7, 1996, p. 3.

96. Penny Morvant, "Russia: Elections Dominate May Day Parades," *OMRI Analytical Brief* 1, no. 98 (May 3, 1996): 1.

97. "Poderzhali Yeltsina," *Nezavisimaya Gazeta*, June 8, 1996.

98. The Foundation for Public Opinion first recorded Yeltsin ahead of Zyuganov in their weekly poll of April 13, when Yeltsin had 23 percent support and Zyuganov had 22. CESSI had the two candidates even in the April 23 poll, whereas the All-Russian Institute for Public Opinion Research (VTsIOM) recorded Yeltsin pulling even with Zyuganov in their May 5 poll.

99. Yeltsin, interview on *Itogi*, NTV, June 9, 1996.

CHAPTER 4

1. Just before these elections, Yeltsin had banned the Communist Party for the second time in as many years. After this ban was lifted, many within the Communist Party still questioned whether they should participate in "Yeltsin's" parliamentary elections, elections seen by most in the party as illegitimate. Although the party eventually did decide to participate, smaller radical parties, including, most importantly, Victor Anpilov's

Working Russia, still urged their followers to boycott the elections. Given the uncertainty of the KPRF's participation (would Yeltsin sanction their participation and would the party vote in favor of it?), several prominent members of the communist faction from the previous parliament decided to join the then newly created Agrarian Party. Although the Agrarian Party was created just before the 1993 elections with the blessing of the KPRF, this friendly defection of candidates and organizers initially weakened the mother party. Moreover, despite the mythology of the KPRF's organizational prowess, links between Moscow and the regions as well as horizontal communications within the party were interrupted and weak in 1993. Financially, the party was broke. Psychologically, the "victory" of Yeltsin over the Congress of People's Deputies in October 1993 led many to believe that communism as a movement and ideology was destined for the "dustbin of history."

2. Each Duma deputy was allowed to hire up to five staff members on a fixed budget provided by the state. Whereas most deputies used this staff and money for their personal affairs such as writing legislation or secretarial assistance, KPRF deputies (as well as LDPR deputies) were required to devote portions of their personal staffs to the party as a whole. As a telling example, the Communist Party appointed Valentin Kuptsov as the chief of staff for the faction. Although most other administrative heads of factions were junior nonpolitical staffers that often served as personal secretaries to faction chairs, Kuptsov was a senior party official (considered by most to be the second-most prominent party boss after Zyuganov) who used the post to strengthen ties between the KPRF Duma faction and party organizers throughout Russia.

3. See Aman Tuleev, "Pochemu ya idu s KPRF?" *Dialog,* nos. 11–12 (1995): 8–9.

4. On Communist Party ties to trade unions, see Evgenii Krasnikov, "Profsoyuzy ishchut vygodnuyu partiyu," *Moskovskie Novosti,* August 6–13, 1995, p. 4. On ties with women's groups, a strategy aimed directly at winning votes away from Women of Russia, see Elena Shubalova, "Russkie Zhenshchiny," *Dialog,* nos. 11–12 (1995): 26–27. Information about ties to the business community comes from the author's interview with Communist Party member and Duma deputy Viktor Zorkaltsev, August 1995; and interview with Zyuganov in *Kommersant'-Daily,* July 6, 1995, p. 4.

5. For details, see Petrov and McFaul, *Politicheskii al'manakh Rossii 1995.*

6. Zyuganov speech before the Fifth Plenum of the KPRF Central Committee, reprinted in *Informatsionnyi byulleten'* (KPRF) 34, no. 1 (January 15, 1996): 3.

7. Ibid.

8. Although personally unhappy with his status within the Duma faction after the December election, Romanov decided to wait until after the presidential election to push his independent line. (Author's interview with Duma deputy Nina Berdnikova, CPRF faction, March 26, 1996.) Tuleev ran as a backup candidate for Zyuganov until days before the first round.

9. Interview with Kuptsov in *Vek,* June 14, 1996, p. 5.

10. Author's interview with Duma deputy Nina Berdnikova, KPRF faction, March 26, 1996.

11. Valerii Mikhalyuk, "Pyat let reforma" (Moskva) VTsIOM, 1996. For instance, in VTsIOM surveys conducted in 1996, 61 percent of respondents stated that they lived best during "zastoi"—the period before 1985— 13 percent cited the period of perestroika, while only 10 percent mentioned the present market period. When asked which economic system is better, the market or the plan, 42 percent said the plan, compared with 35 percent who liked the market better. These figures contrast sharply with answers to the same question asked in 1992, when only 27 percent preferred the planned economy, while 45 percent favored the market.

12. See the opening remarks by Valentin Kuptsov before the Fourth All-Russian Party Conference, reprinted in *Informatsionnyi byulleten'* (KPRF) 35, no. 2 (February 20, 1996): 10.

13. Zyuganov speech before the Fifth Plenum of the KPRF Central Committee, reprinted in *Informatsionnyi byulleten'* (KPRF) 34, no. 1 (January 15, 1996): 4.

14. Kuptsov called this task the main objective of their campaign. See the interview with Kuptsov in *Vek,* June 14, 1996, p. 5.

15. On Zyuganov's ideological evolution, see Veliko Vujacic, "Gennadii Zyuganov and the 'Third Road,'" *Post-Soviet Affairs* 12, no. 2 (April–June 1996): 118–54; and Adrian Karatnycky, "Gennady Zyuganov: Russia's Pragmatist Extremist," *Freedom Review* 27, no. 3 (May/June 1996): 27–40.

16. On Prokhanov and his ideological influence over the Russian Communist Party, see John Dunlop, *The Rise of Russia and the Fall of the Soviet Empire* (Princeton, N.J.: Princeton University Press, 1993), pp. 169–177. On Podberezkin and his organization, see *Shto takoe "Dukhovnoe Nasledie"* (Moskva: "Obozrevatel," 1996).

17. Zyuganov, Interfax, March 31, 1996, quoted here from *Moskovskii Komsomolets,* April 2, 1996, p. 2.

18. Aleksandr Shabanov, deputy chairman of the CPRF, speech at the Moscow Carnegie Center, March 28, 1996.

19. The blend of nationalism and socialism in Serbia may be the only exception.

20. Aleksei Podberezkin, KPRF Duma deputy and one of Zyuganov's chief campaign strategists, remarks at the Carnegie Moscow Center, June 10, 1996. See also Prokhanov's remarks in the *New York Times*, May 2, 1996.

21. Quoted in Viktor Khramaev "Gennadii Zyuganov ob'yavil pobeditelem," *Segodnya*, June 14, 1996, p. 1.

22. Valentin Kuptsov speech to the Fourth All-Russian Party Conference, reprinted in *Informatsionnyi byulleten'* (KPRF) 35, no. 2 (February 20, 1996): 11.

23. Zyuganov, Saint Petersburg, April 27, 1996, as quoted in *OMRI Russian Presidential Election Survey*, no. 2 (May 10, 1996): 9.

24. Zyuganov speech before the fourth party conference, February 15, 1996, reprinted in *Informatsionnyi byulleten'* (KPRF) 35, no. 2 (February 20, 1996): 28. See also O. Shenkarev (KPRF faction coordinator), "O rabote Gosudarstevennoi Dumy v yanvare-febrale 1996 goda," *Informatsionnyi byulleten'* (KPRF) 35, no. 2 (February 20, 1996): 6.

25. Zyuganov speech before agrarian workers, May 31, 1996, cited here from Federal Information Systems Corporation, an electronic service, May 31, 1996, p. 34.

26. Valentin Kuptsov speech to the Fourth All-Russian Party Conference, reprinted in *Informatsionnyi byulleten'* (KPRF) 35, no. 2 (February 20, 1996): 13.

27. Evgenii Maslinin, "Oshibka budet poslednei," *Pravda*, March 28, 1996, p. 1.

28. Zyuganov speech before agrarian workers, May 31, 1996, cited here from Federal Information Systems Corporation, May 31, 1996, p. 34.

29. Zyuganov speech before the fourth party conference, February 15, 1996, reprinted in *Informatsionnyi byulleten'* (KPRF) 35, no. 2, (February 20, 1996): 28.

30. Zyuganov remarks before miners, as quoted in Yurii Nevezhin, "Novyi gost' u shakhterov," *Nezavisimaya Gazeta*, March 30, 1996, p. 2.

31. *OMRI Russian Presidential Election Survey*, no. 5 (May 29, 1996).

32. Valentin Kuptsov, speech to the Fourth All-Russian Party Confer-

ence, reprinted in *Informatsionnyi byulleten'* (KPRF) 35, no. 2 (February 20, 1996): 24.

33. *Rossiya, Rodina, Narod ! Predvybornaya platforma kandidata na post prezidenta rossiiskoi federatsii G.A. Zyuganova,* reprinted in *Zavtra* 120, no. 12 (1996): 3.

34. Author's interview with Duma deputy Nina Berdnikova, KPRF faction, March 26, 1996. Zyuganov, however, did reject the accord as unconstitutional. See his speech before the fourth party conference, February 15, 1996, reprinted in *Informatsionnyi byulleten'* (KPRF) 35, no. 2 (February 20, 1996): 29.

35. Zyuganov speech in Saint Petersburg, April 27, 1996, as quoted in *OMRI Russian Presidential Election Survey,* no. 2 (May 10, 1996): 8.

36. O. Shenkarev (KPRF faction coordinator), "O rabote Gosudarstevennoi Dumy v yanvare-febrale 1996 goda," p. 4; and Zyuganov speech before the fourth party conference, February 15, 1996, in *Informatsionnyi byulleten'* (KPRF) 35, no. 2 (February 20, 1996): 36.

37. Valentin Kuptsov speech to the Fourth All-Russian Party Conference, reprinted in *Informatsionnyi byulleten'* (KPRF) 35, no. 2 (February 20, 1996): 15.

38. Zyuganov speech before the fifth plenum of the KPRF Central Committee, reprinted in *Informatsionnyi byulleten'* (KPRF) 34, no. 1 (January 15, 1996): 8.

39. For an overview, see Michael Gordon, "Russia's Communists Have New, Mixed Manifesto," *New York Times,* May 7, 1996, p. A6.

40. This was the view conveyed to the author in an interview with Duma deputy Anatolii Chekhoyev, deputy chairman of Committee on CIS Affairs, CPRF faction, March 27, 1996.

41. See O. Shenkarev, (KPRF faction coordinator), "O rabote Gosudarstevennoi Dumy v yanvare-febrale 1996 goda," *Informatsionnyi byulleten'* (KPRF) 35, no. 2 (February 20, 1996): 5.

42. Gordon, "Russia's Communists Have New, Mixed Manifesto."

43. *Programma Kommunisticheskoi partii Rossiiskoi Federatsii* (third congress), January 22, 1995 (Moskva: Informpechat' 1995), p. 21.

44. Zyuganov, *Rossiya, Rodina, Narod!*

45. Zyuganov speech before the fourth party conference, February 15, 1996, reprinted in *Informatsionnyi byulleten'* (KPRF) 35, no. 2 (February 20, 1996): 30.

46. See section nine of Zyuganov's economic program, reprinted in

Vozrozhdenie Urala, June 6. 1996, p. 2, and the article by Yurii Maslyukov, KPRF Duma deputy and one of Zyuganov's chief economic advisers, "Nuzhen novyi kurs ekonomicheskikh reform," *Segodnya*, June 14, 1996, p. 3.

47. Zyuganov speech before the fourth party conference, February 15, 1996, reprinted in *Informatsionnyi byulleten'* (KPRF) 35, no. 2 (February 20, 1996): 29.

48. Zyuganov, *Rossiya, Rodina, Narod!*

49. Ibid.

50. Author's interview with Anatolii Chekhoyev, March 27, 1996.

51. "Postanovelnie Plenuma Tsentral'nogo Komiteta Kommunisticheskoi Partii Rossiiskoi Federatsii, "Ob otnoshenii KPRF k konfliktu c Chechne," reprinted in *Informatsionnyi byulleten'* (KPRF) 34, no. 1 (January 15, 1996): 23.

52. Zyuganov, *Rossiya, Rodina, Narod!*

53. *Programma Kommunisticheskoi partii Rossiiskoi Federatsii*, p. 21.

54. Aleksandr Sigal, Pravda correspondent and Duma staff member, KPRF faction, remarks at Carnegie Moscow Center, March 28, 1996.

55. *Programma Kommunisticheskoi partii Rossiiskoi Federatsii*, p. 20.

56. Zyuganov, *Rossiya, Rodina, Narod!*

57. *Nightline*, ABC TV, April 17, 1996.

58. *Programma Kommunisticheskoi partii Rossiiskoi Federatsii*, p. 16.

59. Valentin Kuptsov speech to the fourth party conference, reprinted in *Informatsionnyi byulleten'* (KPRF) 35, no. 2 (February 20, 1996): 23.

60. Zyuganov press conference, broadcast on ORT, March 29, 1996. Commenting on his plans for television should Zyuganov win, Anpilov without hesitation promised to get rid of Jews on television and limit foreign programming to 10 percent. (Anpilov interview on *Itogi*, NTV, June 9, 1996.)

61. *Itogi*, NTV, June 9, 1996.

62. Author's interview with Nikolai Ryzhkov, the head of the bloc, April 1, 1996.

63. Shabanov, remarks at Carnegie Moscow Center conference, "Communist in Contemporary Russia: Who Are They?" March 28, 1996, mimeo, p. 7.

64. "Zyuganov v Omske," *Nezavisimaya Gazeta*, June 8, 1996, p. 2; and Dmitrii Volkov, "Ruka i serdtse KPRF," *Segodnya*, June 5, 1996, p. 2.

65. Tuleev eventually did join the Yeltsin government as minister of CIS affairs.

66. O. Shenkarev (KPRF faction coordinator), "O rabote Gosudarstevennoi Dumy v yanvare-febrale 1996 goda," *Informatsionnyi byulleten'* (KPRF) 35, no. 2 (February 20, 1996): p. 3.

67. Vyacheslav Igrunov, Duma deputy from Yabloko, talk at Stanford University, May 6, 1996. Because all resources of the Duma were controlled by the Communists for campaign purposes, even simple tasks like photocopying were difficult to accomplish for noncommunist members of the legislature. (Author's interview with Duma deputy Galina Staravoitova, June 5, 1996.)

68. Author's interview with Ryzhkov, April 1, 1996.

69. Kuptsov speech to the fourth party conference, reprinted in *Informatsionnyi byulleten'* (KPRF) 35, no. 2 (February 20, 1996): 22.

70. Author's interview (June 20, 1996) with Gleb Cherkasov, reporter from the newspaper *Segodnya* assigned to cover Zyuganov. See also Sergei Chugaev, "Kommunisty ukhodit v glukhuyu oboronu," *Izvestiya*, June 22, 1996, p, 2.

71 "Na teleekrane—tol'ko bogache?" *Pravda*, March 28, 1996, p.1.

72. Author's interview with Maksim Dianov, press secretary for Spiritual Heritage, July 6, 1996.

73. See Zudin, "Biznes i politika v prezidentskoi kampanii 1996 goda," *Pro et Contra* 1, no. 1 (fall 1996): 47. For official sources of funding for the Zyuganov campaign, see "Tsentral'noi Izbiratel'noi Komissii Rossiiskoi Federatsii," *Vestnik* 37, no. 17 (1996): 54–55.

CHAPTER 5

1. Sergei Markov, "June Vote: Not Just a Two-Horse Race," *Moscow Times*, May 5, 1996, p. 8.

2. Author's interview with Duma deputy Vyacheslav Igrunov, Yabloko, March 28, 1996.

3. *OMRI Daily Digest*, no. 89 (May 7, 1996): part 1, p. 1.

4. Quoted in John Helmer, "Can Yeltsin Win the Elections on Lebed's Coattails?" *Moscow Tribune*, June 20, 1996, p. 1. The phrase "I know such a person" was a famous line from Lebed's television commercials, making it clear to political observers to whom Yeltsin was referring.

5. Author's interview with General Shevtsov, executive chairman of the political organization Chest i Sovest', December 17, 1996.

6. Golovkov served as campaign director. Leonid Radzikhovskii, a former Democratic Russia activist, wrote Lebed's campaign speeches and slogans. Yuliya Rusova, a well-respected campaign organizer and close colleague of Golovkov's, handled agitation, direct mail, and image making. Vitalii Naishul, a neoliberal economist, wrote Lebed's economic program, though Sergei Glaziev, a running mate of Lebed's from the 1995 parliamentary elections, wrote a more conservative economic program for the general. According to Rusova, her team of consultants made most campaign decisions in consultation with Lebed. Lebed's former advisers and allies played a secondary role in the campaign, did not trust this group of "Yeltsin spies," and quickly pushed the consultants away from Lebed the day after the election. (Author's interview with Rusova, July 5, 1996.)

7. In an interview with the author (September 18, 1996), Dmitrii Rogozin estimated that Inkombank financed 40 percent of Lebed's entire campaign budget.

8. For details on Lebed's 1995 performance, see McFaul, *Russia between Elections.*

9. Vitalii Tretyakov, "Russkaya Ruletka: Vybory 16 yunya," *Nezavisimaya Gazeta,* June 14, 1996, p. 3.

10. One was written by Sergei Glaziev, the leading opposition economist in the Duma. Neoliberal Vitalii Naishul penned the other. According to campaign managers from Golovkov's team, Lebed did not understand the differences between the two programs. (Author's interviews with Igor Dubov and Yuliya Rusova, December 15, 1996.)

11. Aleksandr Lebed, "Pravda i poryadok" (campaign leaflet, 1996), p. 3.

12. Lebed, interview on *Itogi,* NTV, June 9, 1996.

13. Yavlinsky grossly misplayed the 1995 elections. During the summer of 1995, Yavlinsky deliberately distanced himself from Gaidar's Democratic Choice of Russia and the other "democrats" who, in Yavlinsky's view, were tainted by their past mistakes. According to Yavlinsky, "the polls say that if I join Mr. Gaidar I will lose 46 percent of my voters." (Quoted in Alessandra Stanley, "A Russian Reformer with Rough Edges," *New York Times,* December 1, 1995, p. 1.) Instead, Yavlinsky decided to use the 1995 parliamentary elections as a primary for the 1996 presidential race. If he won a greater percentage of the vote than all other democratic leaders in 1995, Yavlinsky reasoned that he could call on all democratic forces to unite behind him in 1996. (Grigorii Yavlinsky, "V paskole demokratov tragedii net," *Izvestiya,* July 13, 1995, part 2, p. 2.) After he fared

so miserably in the 1995 elections, however, few "reformist" parties or financial backers of reform were willing to support him.

14. Talk by Yabloko Duma deputy Vyacheslav Igrunov at Stanford, May 6, 1996; and author's interview with Yabloko Duma deputy Ivan Grachev, March 26, 1996.

15. Author's interview with Pyotr Shelesh, March 26, 1996.

16. See the VTsIOM data comparing 1995 preferences with 1996 preferences presented by Andrei Klochkov, Hadezhda Antoshchina, and Andrei Savel'ev, in *Vestnik Fonda* (Moskva: Rossiiskii Obshchestvenno-Politicheskii Tsentr, May 1996), p. 41.

17. Richard Sleder, "Prominent Liberals Support Yavlinsky," *Moscow Tribune*, April 2, 1996, p.5.

18. The author saw virtually every television advertisement aired in the 1996 election, including all Yavlinsky's paid spots.

19. Makhman Gafarly, "Idet poisk novykh podkhodov," *Nezavisimaya Gazeta*, March 30, 1996, p. 3; "Zayevlenie fraktsii 'Yabloko,'" *Yabloko*, Spetsial'nyi vypusk, March 1996, p. 1.

20. *OMRI Daily Digest*, no. 93 (May 14,1996): part 1.

21. *OMRI Russian Presidential Election Survey*, no. 5 (May 29, 1996).

22. Author's interview with LDPR leader and Duma deputy Aleksei Mitrofanov, April 1, 1996.

23. According to Aleksei Mitrofanov in an interview with the author September 16, 1996, the LDPR was much more active in 1995 than in 1996, in part because individual party leaders had personal incentives (i.e., seats in the Duma) to campaign in 1995 but few incentives in 1996 and in part because Zhirinovsky himself was much more animated in the parliamentary race than in the presidential election.

24. Anatolii Veslo, "Vladimir Zhirinovskii ozabotilsya spaseniem Borisa Yeltsina," *Segodnya*, June 5, 1996, p. 2.

25. Ibid., p. 2.

26. *OMRI Daily Digest*, no. 105 (May 30, 1996): part 1.

27. Author's interview (March 30, 1996) with a colonel in Korzhakov's "analytical center" who asked not to be identified; and LDPR Duma deputy and campaign strategist Aleksei Mitrofanov, September 16, 1996. According to Mitrofanov, Zhirinovsky would have been named minister for social policy in Yeltsin's new government had Korzhakov and Soskovets not been dismissed.

28. After the first round, Zhirinovsky contended that Zyuganov could

have won had his patriotic bloc included the LDPR (Zhirinovsky, June 14, 1996, MTV, channel 6).

29. Zhirinovsky public address, June 12, 1996. See also Viktoriya Shokhina, "Za Vladimira Zhirinovskogo," *Nezavisimaya Gazeta*, June 14, 1996, p. 4; and Mukhin, Zapeklyi, and Tyukov, *Rossiya: Presidenskaya Kampaniya*, p. 49.

30. *OMRI Russian Presidential Election Survey*, no. 1 (May 3, 1996): 4.

31. *Monitor—a Daily Briefing on the Post-Soviet States* 2, no. 103 (May 24, 1996).

32. *OMRI Russian Presidential Election Survey*, no. 2 (May 10, 1996): 5.

33. Former senior official in the LDPR Aleksandr Vengerovskii claimed in an interview with *Izvestiya* on May 13 that half the Duma deputies representing Vladimir Zhirinovsky's Liberal Democratic Party of Russia (LDPR) bought their places on the party list for an average of $1 million.

34. See the interview with NTV general director Igor Malashenko in *Nezavisimaya Gazeta*, March 30, 1996, p. 5.

35. Author's interviews with members of Gorbachev's campaign team, July 5, 1996.

CHAPTER 6

1. Author's interviews with Vladimir Zharikin and Valerii Khomyakov, Yeltsin campaign organizers, June 19, 1996.

2. VTsIOM, *Prezidentskie vybory 1996 goda i obshchestvennoe mnenie* (Moskva: VTsIOM, 1996), p. 70.

3. From "Realizatsiya kampanii pervogo tura golosvaniya," mimeo, Yeltsin campaign headquarters, 1996.

4. See especially, Institute of Ethnology and Anthropology, Russian Academy of Science, *Ekspess-Analiz rezultatov pervogo tura golosolvaniya, spetsial'nyi vypusk* (Moscow: June 16, 1996).

5. For a detailed chronology of actions taken by both Yeltsin and Zyuganov between rounds, see Aleksei Titkov, "Regional'naya kompaniya mezhdu turami," *Prezidentskie vybory v Rossii*, no. 10 (Moscow Carnegie Center) (July 1996).

6. Between rounds, Aleksandr Oslon and the Foundation of Public Opinion identified through exit polling a special category within the electorate called "new supporters of Yeltsin." Although 65 percent of the public as whole approved of Lebed's appointment, 82 percent of these new potential voters supported the move. These figures come from Fond

'Obshchestvennoe mnenie', "Novye storoniki B. Yeltsina," *Rezultaty sotsiologicheskikh isledovanii,* no. 110 (June 25, 1996): 3.

7. Fond 'Obshchestvennoe mnenie', *Rezultaty sotsiologicheskikh isledovanii,* no. 67 (June 5, 1996): 2.

8. Ilya Bulavinov, "Rekomenduetsya bol'she trekh ne sobirat'sya," *Kommersant'-Daily,* June 20, 1996, p. 3.

9. Alexander Lebed, "My Only Personal Dedications Is to Russia," *Moscow Tribune,* June 22, 1996, p. 6.

10. Ibid.

11. Hough, Davidheiser, and Lehmann, *The 1996 Russian Presidential Election,* p. 103; John Helmer, "Lebed Gains Could Be a Mirage," *Moscow Tribune,* June 19, 1996, p. 1; Viktor Ilyukhin, KPRF Duma deputy, as quoted in "The Lebed Factor," *Moscow Times,* June 22, 1996, p. 9; and Stephen Cohen remarks on the *Charlie Rose Show,* PBS television, transcript, June 17, 1996.

12. See Vladimir Bokser, Michael McFaul, and Vasilii Ostavshev, "Elektoraty priserov," *Prezidentskie Vybory v Rossii,* no. 9 (June 1996): 5–8; Aleksandr Sobyanin and Vladislav Sukovol'skii, "Izbirateli razdelilis' ne tri pochti ravnye chasti," *Presidentskie vybory v Rossii,* no. 9 (Moscow, Carnegie Center) (June 1996): 9–11.

13. Igor Klyamkin, "Politicheskie predpochteniya pazlichnykh sotsial'no-professional'nikh grupp rossiiskogo obshchestva na parlamenskikh vyborakh 1995 goda," ms., Moscow Carnegie Center, February 1996.

14. Interview with Aman Tuleev in *Pravda,* June 22, 1996, p. 3.

15. Dmitrii Polikarpov, "Poll Says Lebed Alliance Boosts Yeltsin's Chances, *Moscow Tribune,* June 26, 1996, p. 1. See also Leonti Byzov, "Novyi Peredel golosov," *Obshchaya Gazeta,* June 20–26, 1996, p. 8.

16. Aleksandr Oslon, president of FPO, press conference, June 28, 1996.

17. "Esli bol'shinsvto ne pridet, to pobedit men'shinstvo," *Kommersant'-Daily,* July 1, 1996, p. 3.

18. See Natalya Arkhangelskaya, "Nikakoi podderzhki kommunistam," *Kommersant'-Daily,* June 25, 1996, p. 3; and Dmitrii Volkov, "Grigorii Yavlinskii prizval Borisa Yeltsina k otvetu," *Segodnya,* June 26, 1996, p. 2.

19. Quoted in Matt Bivens, "Chubais Rules Out Post in Cabinet," *Moscow Times,* July 6, 1996, p. 3.

20. Author's conversation with Yavlinsky, July 1, 1996.

21. Fond "Obshchestvennoe mnenie," *Rezultaty sotsiologicheskikh issledovannii*, no. 67 (June 5, 1996): 4.

22. Author's interviews with Yeltsin campaign officials, June 1996. The author confirmed this practice in private conversations with two Dagestani citizens.

23. Andrei Zhukov, "The Election, Viewed through the Prism of Regional Voting Preferences," *Prism: A Monthly of the Post-Soviet States* 2 (July 1996): part 3.

24. "Esli bol'shinsvto ne pridet, to pobedit men'shinstvo," *Kommersant'-Daily*, July 1, 1996, p. 3.

25. Fond "Obshchestvennoe mnenie,' "Klyuchevie problemy kampanii vtorgo tura," *Rezultaty sotsiologicheskikh isledovanii*," no. 98 (June 21, 1996): 1.

26. Natal'ya Arkhangelskaya, "Organisatsiya b'et klass," *Kommersant'-Daily*, June 28, 1996, p. 3.

27. In Moscow, Ivan Rybkin, Boris Fyodorov, and Sergei Shakrai announced the creation of a new democratic union of small reformist parties. Yeltsin also created a new "social chamber," chaired by Rybkin, to give parties and organizations not represented in the Duma a voice in governmental affairs. These unifying acts, however, did not have the resonance in society originally planned by the campaign, as they were not followed by similar acts of consolidation in the regions.

28. According to several Yeltsin campaign officials interviewed by the author, the White House served as a safe place for campaign money raised by Chubais; other places, such as the Presidential Hotel or the Kremlin, were controlled by Korzhakov.

29. Quoted from the *New York Times*, May 13, 1996.

30. Christina Ling, "Bomb Blast Rips Moscow Metro Train, Kills 4," *Moscow Tribune*, June 13, 1996, p. 1.

31. Several analysts and government officials have speculated that these arrests were the beginning of a palace coup. Allegedly, Chubais and several bankers expected to be arrested next. For the story, see David Remnick, "The War for the Kremlin," *New Yorker*, July 22, 1996.

32. Konstantin Molchanov, "Tret'e Yulya," *Pravda*, June 20, 1996.

33. Gleb Cherkasov, "Kommunisty sokhranyayut prisutvie dukha," *Segodnya*, June 18, 1996, p. 2.

34. Author's interviews with numerous CPRF officials, July 1996. See also the remarks by Aleksei Podberezkin in Richard Boudreaux, "Zyuganov Erred in Courting Nationalists," *Los Angeles Times*, June 17, 1996.

35. Some have argued that Zyuganov and his allies won 51 percent of the vote in 1995. This explains why these analysts predicted a communist victory in 1996. This assessment of the 1995 results, however, was flawed. Even by their own assessment, the KPRF victory in 1995 was not as sweeping as reported in the West. According to campaign chairman Valentin Kuptsov, the "leftist, national-patriotic forces" won 32 percent of the popular vote in 1995. Valentin Kuptsov speech to the Fourth All-Russian Party Conference, reprinted in *Informatsionnyi byulleten'* (KPRF) 35, no. 2 (February 20, 1996): 15.

36. Quoted in John Helmer, "Can Yeltsin Win the Elections on Lebed's Coattails?" *Moscow Tribune,* June 20, 1996, p. 1.

37. Interview with Kuptsov in *Vek,* June 14, 1996, p. 5.

38. Jonas Bernstein, "Yeltsin's Huge Lead Doubted by Pollsters," *Moscow Times,* June 29, 1996, p. 3.

39. Author's interview with CPRF campaign adviser Vladimir Akimov, July 1, 1996.

40. Comment by Andrei Fyodorov, aide to Rutskoi, at the Moscow Carnegie Center, June 19, 1996. For an analysis of this strategy, see Sergei Chugaev, "Kommunisty ukhodit v glukhuyu oboronu," *Izvestiya,* June 22, 1996, p. 2.

41. Marina Shakina, "Zyuganov predlozhil kompromiss," *Nezavisimaya Gazeta,* June 26, 1996, p. 2.

42. Evgenii Yur'ev, "Zyuganov gotovit Ledebyu 'khoroshuyu dolzhnost,'" *Kommersant'-Daily,* June 20, 1996, p. 3.

43. Matt Bivens, "Zyuganov Unveils 'Healthy Coalition'" *Moscow Times,* June 25, 1996, p. 1.

44. Sergei Chugaev, "Kommunisty ukhodit v glukhuyu oboronu," *Izvestiya,* June 22, 1996, p, 2.

45. Interview with Andreeva and Terekov, *Itogi,* NTV television, June 30, 1996.

46. Tuleev, *Itogi,* NTV television, June 30, 1996.

47. I. Lopatin, "Kogda zaverbovali krutogo generala," *Sovetskaya Rossiya,* June 26, 1996, p. 6; and Antonina Korzinina, "Kak odin general vsekh zhenshchin 'obmanul,'" *Sovetskaya Rossiya,* June 22, 1996, p. 3. This article, allegedly written by a trade union leader from Ivanova, was aimed specifically at the large number of working-class women in Ivanova who voted for Lebed, a city where the general received an amazing 30 percent of the vote.

48. Kontantin Molchanov, "Tretii putsh' Borisa Yeltsina," *Sovetskaya Rossiya*, June 22, 1996, p. 5.

49. See Vasilii Safronchuk, "Kupit li Chubais zhivye dyshi?" *Sovetskaya Rossiya*, June 27, 1996, p. 6.

50. Author's conversations with Sergei Blagovolin, director of ORT, and Aleksei Pushkov, deputy director, July 5, 1996.

51. See the quote by Zyuganov in Ivan Rodin, "Oppositsiya," *Nezavisimaya Gazeta*, June 26, 1996, p. 2.

52. For an analysis, see the articles by Bokser, McFaul, and Ostashev; Sobyanin; and Petrov in *Prezidentskie vybory v Rossii*, no. 10 (Moscow Carnegie Center) (July 1996).

53. Yeltsin won 565,000 more votes in Tatarstan than Zyuganov, the fifth-largest victory margin for Yeltsin after Moscow, Sverdlovsk, Saint Petersburg, and Moscow Oblast.

54. Yeltsin performed extremely well in Chechnya-Ingushetiya in 1991 by promising to resolve the border dispute with Georgia in favor of the Russian republic. After Yeltsin failed to resolve this dispute in a way favorable to Ingushetiya, his popularity fell rapidly, as demonstrated by his poor showing there in referenda votes in 1993.

55. Tsentral'naya Izbiratel'naya Kommissiya Rossiiskaya Federatsiya, *Vybory Prezidenta Rossiiskoi Federatsii 1996: Elektoral'naya Statistika* (Moskva: TsIK, 1996), pp. 184–85.

56. Figures quoted from VTsIOM, *Prezidentskie vybory 1996 goda i obshchestvennoe mnenie* (Moskva: VTsIOM, 1996), p. 54.

57. Ibid.

58. VTsIOM, "Ekpress 96-20," July 9–12, 1996, 1,588 respondents, mimeo. Unfortunately, this poll did not disaggregate these income groups more specifically.

59. Tsentral'naya Izbiratel'naya Kommissiya Rossiiskaya Federatsiya, *Vybory Prezidenta Rossiiskoi Federatsii 1996: Elektoral'naya Statistika* (Moskva: TsIK, 1996), p. 204.

60. Zyuganov, as quoted in the *Moscow Tribune*, July 5, 1996, p. 2.

61. Valentin Kuptsov, CPRF campaign manager, press conference, June 4, 1996, transcribed and translated by Federal Information Systems Corporation, p. 19.

62. Author's interview with Aleksandr Sovolev, legal adviser, CPRF Duma staff, December 18, 1996.

63. William Zimmerman, "Foreign Policy, Political System Preference,

and the Russian Presidential Election of 1996," AAASS paper, November 16, 1996, p. 8.

64. Quoted in John Thornhill, "Masterly Performance from Ailing President," *Financial Times,* July 5, 1996, p. 2.

65. Author's interview with CPRF campaign strategist Vladimir Akimov, July 5, 1996.

66. Quoted in Chrystia Freeland, "Communists Accept Defeat like Democrats," *Financial Times,* July 5, 1996, p. 2.

CHAPTER 7

1. On the wage arrears problem and taxation, see Gennady Melikyan, "Causes of Social Instability," *Executive and Legislative Newsletter,* no. 45 (1996). In the first ten months of 1996, Russia's GDP fell by 6 percent and industrial output fell by 5 percent compared with last year. From January through October, the volume of investment totaled 247 trillion rubles, 18 trillion less than the same period in 1995. The number of unemployed also increased to 11 percent. These figures come from ITAR-TASS as reported in *OMRI Daily Digest,* no. 222 (November 15, 1996): part 1.

2. Speech by Gromov in the State Duma, reprinted in *Sovetskaya Rossiya,* October 31, 1996.

3. Quoted in *Segodnya,* November 13, 1996.

4. Lebed, interview on the *Newshour with Jim Lehrer,* November 23, 1996. See also Andrei Koliev, "The Army's Patience Is Running Out," *Prism: A Monthly on the Post-Soviet States* 2 (November 1996): part 1.

5. The model here is the accord signed by the leaders of Russia, Ukraine, and Belarus in December 1991 that effectively dissolved the USSR.

6. See Anna Paretskaya, "Russian Central Authorities Seek New Formula for Relations with the Regions," *OMRI Analytical Brief,* no. 460 (November 13, 1996).

7. This poll was conducted by the All-Russia Opinion Research Center and reported by the Associated Press, November 13, 1996.

8. Yurii Levada, director of VTsIOM, public lecture at the AAASS Convention, Boston, November 16, 1996.

9. The distinctions drawn here between political, economic, and civil societies are borrowed from Larry Diamond, "Toward Democratic Consolidation," *Journal of Democracy* 5, no. 3 (July 1994): 4–17.

10. Liliya Shevtsova, *Postkommunisticheskaya Rossiya: logika razvitiya i per-*

skepti (Moscow: Moscow Carnegie Center, 1995). On systems of interest mediation, see Philippe Schmitter, "The Consolidation of Democracy and Representation of Social Groups," *American Behavioral Scientist* 35, nos. 4 and 5 (March/June 1992): 422–49.

11. "Bolshoi vos'merke' vybory ne nuzhny," *Kommersant'-Daily*, March 14, 1995, p. 3.

12. The most important new alliance formed during the presidential election was between Vladimir Gusinskii, owner of Most Bank and the NTV television network (channel 4), and Boris Berezovskii, head of Logovaz and chairman of the board of the ORT television network (channel 1). Before the elections, the consortium of banks and businesses allied with Berezovskii, the so-called big eight, had been at odds with Gusinskii. Berezovskii was deeply tied to the national state, whereas Gusinskii dominated Luzhkov's Moscow government. These distinctions between "All-Russian" businesses and "Moscow" groups have become more blurred since July.

13. Freeland, Thornhill, and Gowers, "Moscow's Group of Seven."

14. Lijphart, "Presidentialism and Majoritarian Democracy."

15. On the relationship between proportional representation and multiparty systems, see Shugart and Carey, *Presidents and Assemblies*; and Sartori, *Comparative Constitutional Engineering*. On Duma factions, see Thomas Remington and Steven Smith, "The Development of Parliamentary Parties in Russia," *Legislative Studies Quarterly* 20 (1995): 457–89.

16. Since the presidential elections, tensions have arisen between Chernomyrdin, the formal leader of the organization, and Our Home's parliamentary leader Sergei Belyaev. Whereas Belyaev wants to transform Our Home into a political party, Chernomyrdin and his government aides prefer to see the organization as the government's faction in the Duma and nothing more.

17. Yabloko has a significant presence in Saint Petersburg but only scattered support elsewhere. Significantly, in the fifty gubernatorial elections conducted during the fall of 1996, Yabloko ran only an handful of candidates and won only one race.

18. Linz, "Presidential or Parliamentary Democracy."

19. The Communist Party and its bloc ally, the National Patriotic Union of Russia, publicly endorsed only eleven out of fifty-two candidates. Our Home Is Russia also supported several candidates, but only a few were "party" members. No other party ran serious candidates but instead endorsed already competing independents.

20. Darrell Slider, "Elections to Russia's Regional Assemblies," *Post-Soviet Affairs* 12 (1996): 1–21.

21. Peter Ordeshook, "Federal Stability, Political Parties, and Russia," ms., Caltech, February 1996.

22. See Michael McFaul, "Russian Centrism and Revolutionary Transitions" *Post-Soviet Affairs* 9, no. 4 (July–September 1993): 196–222.

23. Anders Aslund, "Governing by Default," *Moscow Times*, November 10, 1996.

24. Conner, *Tattered Banners;* Leonid Gordon, *Oblast' Vozmozhnogo* (Moskva: "Mirt," 1995).

25. See Mark Beissinger, "Protest Mobilization in the Former Soviet Union: Issues and Event Analysis," ms., University of Wisconsin at Madison, June 1995; and William Reisinger, Arthur Miller, and Vicki Hesli, "Political Behavior and Political Change in Post-Soviet States," *Journal of Politics* 57, no. 4 (November 1995): 941–70.

26. Marcia Weigle and Jim Butterfield, "Civil Society in Reforming Communist Regimes," *Comparative Politics* 25, no. 1 (October 1992): 1–23.

27. This observation is based on the author's work as an adviser to the National Democratic Institute (NDI) from 1990 to 1996. During this period, one of NDI's central objectives in Russia was to foster cooperation between civic groups and political parties.

28. This relationship between state and society is similar to the Polish situation throughout the 1980s.

29. On decreasing levels of participation in political and civic activities as a whole, see *Politicheskii Protsess v Rossii v 1994 g: Sotsial'nyi Kontekst i Problemy Politichekogo Uchastiya* (Moscow: Russian Independent Institute for Social and National Problems, 1995).

30. The period of rapid industrialization in the United States at the end of the nineteenth century and the beginning of the twentieth looks like an apt analogue.

31. Robert Dahl, *Polyarchy: Participation and Opposition* (New Haven, Conn.: Yale University Press, 1971); Dietrich Rueschemeyer, Evelyne Huber Stevens, and John D. Stephens, *Capitalist Development and Democracy* (Chicago: University of Chicago Press, 1992).

32. On the importance of the civil code, see David Hoffman, "Russia Gets New Laws for Free Market," *Washington Post*, March 1, 1996, p. 1.

33. This relationship between Russian and foreign capital is often misunderstood in the West. Russia's banks and resource exporters welcome

foreign investment in their business operations, provided that it never approaches a controlling share. They do not want to create circumstances, however, in which foreign capital can enter Russian markets independently and compete with Russian enterprises.

34. It must be remembered that seventy years of Soviet communism has created greater expectations of the state in Russia than in developed capitalist societies.

35. This relationship between elections and interests closely approximates O'Donnell's "delegative democracy." See Guillermo O'Donnell, "Delegative Democracy," *Journal of Democracy* 5, no.1 (January 1994): 55–69.

36. Aslund, "Governing by Default."

37. Mikhail Gorbachev, *Memoirs* (New York: Doubleday, 1996), p. 590.

38. Peter Kirkow, "Regional Warlordism in Russia: The Case of Primorskii Krai," *Europe-Asia Studies* 47, no. 2 (spring 1995): 923–49.

39. The historical analogue in the history of the United States is the election of Theodore Roosevelt.

40. Przeworski has labeled this distinguishing characteristic of democracy *conditional uncertainty*. See Adam Przeworski, "Democracy as a Contingent Outcome of Conflicts," in Jon Elster and Rune Slagstad, eds., *Constitutionalism and Democracy* (Cambridge: Cambridge University Press, 1993), pp. 59–80.

41. Only a handful of these races was cast as "communist" versus "anticommunist"; the vast majority were devoid of ideological content altogether. In some elections Communists and the party of power backed the same candidate. In others the party of power backed competing candidates. In other elections, such as in Leningrad Oblast, Yabloko and the Communists cooperated and backed the same winning candidate. Weeks later, the Communists teamed with the LDPR to back the same candidate in Pskov Oblast.

Appendixes

The author is indebted to Nikolai Petrov and Aleksei Titkov for assistance in preparing these tables.

Appendix 1 Electoral Profiles of Russian Regions

Regions	Share in number of voters, %	Urban population, %	Average age	Turn-out in 1995, %	Votes for "demo-crats" and cen-trists in 1995, %	Votes for leftists and nation-alists in 1995, %
Adygeia	0.31	53.8	36.0	64.2	27.9	51.5
Altay	0.12	23.7	34.0	75.5	33.0	48.9
Bashkortostan	2.62	64.6	33.4	73.8	40.5	49.7
Buryatia	0.63	59.4	30.0	63.8	37.5	46.8
Dagestan	1.07	42.1	28.0	72.4	41.8	53.9
Ingushetia	0.11	29.7	29.3	57.2	84.7	8.8
Kabardino-Balkaria	0.47	59.7	31.5	68.1	46.0	44.8
Kalmykia	0.18	37.8	29.2	67.4	42.3	42.0
Karachayevo-Cherkessia	0.27	47.6	32.4	61.6	28.4	51.1
Kareiia	0.53	74.3	33.3	63.4	57.4	21.4
Komi	0.74	74.9	30.2	56.0	53.6	20.5
Mariy El	0.51	62.2	33.0	66.6	37.1	34.4
Mordovia	0.64	58.6	35.7	67.2	35.8	35.7
Northern Ossetia	0.39	69.5	33.7	63.0	21.2	61.0
Sakha (Yakutia)	0.55	64.5	27.6	65.9	50.5	32.9
Tatarstan	2.47	73.4	34.1	59.2	61.4	27.2
Tuva	0.15	48.1	26.1	65.7	61.3	28.4
Udmurtia	1.06	69.9	32.7	57.6	45.2	33.5
Khakassia	0.36	72.6	32.4	57.6	42.4	32.6
Chechnya	0.46	37.2	29.3	62.1	72.1	17.5
Chuvashia	1.81	52.1	30.4	67.0	31.1	45.5
Altayskiy kray	3.52	54.2	36.6	60.5	33.9	35.9
Krasnodar kray	1.96	73.7	32.2	64.7	44.2	28.6
Krasnoyarsk kray	1.44	77.7	31.8	62.2	38.4	25.4
Primorskiy kray	1.72	53.7	34.6	67.2	31.5	39.8
Stavropol kray	1.02	80.7	31.2	64.5	48.9	24.3
Khabarovsk kray	0.88	60.4	33.4	61.0	32.3	47.6
Amur oblast	0.64	66.3	30.5	67.4	29.9	45.1
Arkhangelsk oblast	0.98	73.4	32.8	65.0	59.0	22.1
Astrakhan oblast	0.68	67.0	33.7	62.0	41.9	33.2
Belgorad oblast	1.01	64.5	37.2	75.5	30.2	45.7
Bryansk oblast	1.03	68.3	37.0	69.4	28.0	44.5
Vladimir oblast	1.14	80.1	36.6	66.4	46.9	28.4
Volgograd oblast	1.84	74.3	36.1	65.1	39.0	37.5
Vologda oblast	0.91	67.2	35.3	64.2	49.9	25.5

Regions	Share in number of voters, %	Urban popula- tion, %	Average age	Turn- out in 1995, %	Votes for "demo- crats" and cen- trists in 1995, %	Votes for leftists and nation- alists in 1995, %
Voronezh oblast	1.82	61.5	38.6	68.1	33.7	39.4
Ivanovo oblast	0.88	82.3	37.7	67.0	46.8	26.5
Irkutsk oblast	1.66	79.4	31.6	58.4	48.9	27.2
Kaliningrad oblast	0.66	78.1	34.1	63.8	48.5	25.8
Kaluga oblast	0.76	73.6	36.5	68.2	41.3	37.0
Kamchatka oblast	0.25	80.8	28.7	60.9	57.9	17.1
Kemerovo oblast	2.01	86.8	34.1	61.1	30.0	52.4
Kirov oblast	1.11	70.2	35.7	68.8	41.3	33.4
Kostroma oblast	0.55	66.1	36.9	68.6	41.0	34.8
Kurgan oblast	0.72	54.8	34.7	69.6	33.2	39.0
Kursk oblast	0.94	59.9	38.1	71.6	22.1	36.5
Leningrad oblast	1.25	66.0	35.8	61.8	51.3	29.5
Lipetsk oblast	0.87	63.3	37.3	65.0	31.1	40.7
Magadan oblast	0.15	87.0	28.5	60.3	49.7	17.1
Moscow oblast	5.12	79.7	36.7	63.2	55.1	27.8
Murmansk oblast	0.74	92.4	30.2	60.9	60.6	15.3
Nizhiny Novgorod oblast	2.65	77.8	37.3	62.4	48.1	28.5
Novgorod oblast	0.52	70.8	37.1	67.2	49.1	28.7
Novosibirsk oblast	1.88	73.8	34.3	66.7	40.5	32.2
Omsk oblast	1.40	67.4	32.6	68.4	39.2	35.7
Orenburg oblast	1.46	64.1	33.5	65.0	38.7	40.0
Oryol oblast	0.64	62.7	37.6	70.5	27.0	54.5
Penza oblast	1.08	64.0	36.7	70.5	30.4	50.2
Perm oblast	1.86	76.4	33.9	58.6	58.1	19.5
Pskov oblast	0.59	65.1	38.2	73.4	36.2	33.5
Rostov oblast	3.03	68.0	36.2	67.5	41.2	36.1
Ryazan oblast	0.95	67.8	38.4	70.2	32.7	43.7
Samara oblast	2.26	73.0	35.1	63.6	47.2	31.2
Saratov oblast	1.88	73.0	35.6	68.1	32.7	39.5
Sakhalin oblast	0.42	85.1	30.8	57.8	42.7	31.7
Sverdlovsk oblast	3.17	87.6	34.7	53.1	65.7	17.0
Smolensk oblast	0.82	69.6	37.1	68.5	29.3	41.8
Tambov oblast	0.90	57.5	38.4	68.6	27.5	52.8
Tver oblast	1.15	72.4	38.4	71.0	39.0	39.7
Tomsk oblast	0.69	65.3	31.8	62.9	50.1	27.1
Tula oblast	1.34	81.3	38.9	68.0	39.5	32.2
Tyumen oblast	0.84	76.1	28.6	61.3	44.3	33.8
Ulyanovsk oblast	1.01	72.6	35.0	66.3	31.6	47.8

Regions	Share in number of voters, %	Urban popula- tion, %	Average age	Turn- out in 1995, %	Votes for "demo- crats" and cen- trists in 1995, %	Votes for leftists and nation- alists in 1995, %
Chelyabinsk oblast	2.46	81.3	34.5	62.8	53.4	24.4
Chita oblast	0.75	63.1	30.2	64.0	32.7	38.9
Yaroslavl oblast	1.02	80.8	37.3	68.3	52.4	23.5
Moscow City	6.53	100.0	37.5	62.8	71.2	17.2
St. Petersburg City	3.46	100.0	36.7	60.5	69.4	18.4
Jewish aut. oblast	0.13	67.3	30.5	63.9	41.2	38.8
Aginskoye Buryat aut. okrug	0.04	32.4	26.8	71.1	23.0	62.5
Korm Permyak aut. okrug	0.09	30.2	33.5	62.3	41.8	28.2
Koryak aut. okrug	0.02	24.3	28.3	65.9	60.0	16.9
Nenets aut. okrug	0.03	60.0	28.5	74.7	54.6	20.7
Taimyr aut. okrug	0.03	66.2	27.4	59.7	63.6	10.5
Ust-Ordynskiy aut. okrug	0.08	100.0	29.5	70.1	34.7	53.1
Khanty-Mansi aut. okrug	0.76	91.5	26.0	54.7	63.4	12.6
Chukotka aut. okrug	0.06	70.6	27.7	66.8	61.9	15.6
Evenk aut. okrug	0.01	28.4	27.0	62.0	51.5	21.0
Yamato-Nenets aut. okrug	0.28	82.9	25.7	61.0	68.8	8.7
RUSSIA TOTAL	100.00	73.0	34.7	64.4	45.5	32.8

Appendix 2 Results of the First Round, June 18, 1996

Macroregions and regions	Number of voters, thousands	Turnout, %	VOTERS FOR					Voters against all candidates
			Yeltsin	Zhirinovsky	Zyuganov	Lebed	Yavlinskiy	
Yakutia	612.0	72.0	51.9	3.7	20.6	12.6	4.7	1.7
Koryak aut. okrug	21.8	72.6	46.0	6.5	15.0	15.8	8.9	2.9
Chukotka aut. okrug	58.8	73.1	48.5	7.6	13.5	17.1	6.4	2.6
Evenk aut. okrug	12.9	65.5	43.4	7.0	20.0	16.4	6.3	1.9
Northern East	705.6	72.0	51.2	4.1	19.8	13.2	5.0	1.8
Primorskiy kray	1,580.0	66.1	29.5	12.7	24.6	19.5	7.2	2.3
Khabarovsk kray	1,103.9	67.0	39.0	8.7	22.9	12.2	10.4	2.2
Kamchatka oblast	272.8	61.4	34.3	10.0	18.7	14.1	17.3	2.3
Magadan oblast	170.1	64.8	36.9	10.9	16.0	23.9	6.1	2.4
Sakhalin oblast	462.2	63.5	29.9	9.1	26.9	18.7	9.3	2.1
Maritime	3,588.9	65.6	33.2	10.7	23.5	16.9	9.1	2.2
Krasnoyarsk kray	2,141.7	70.2	34.8	7.6	28.5	13.9	10.0	1.8
Irkutsk oblast	1,798.8	62.8	32.2	8.5	27.6	16.3	8.9	1.7
Tomsk oblast	745.3	68.7	34.9	7.1	22.1	19.7	10.9	1.6
Tyumen oblast	907.8	67.2	39.1	9.4	27.3	13.3	5.7	1.8
Cheliabinsk oblast	2,663.8	70.3	36.6	5.2	24.7	19.8	8.8	1.4
Middle Siberia	8,257.4	68.1	35.4	7.1	26.4	16.8	9.0	1.6
Perm Oblast	2,020.0	66.6	55.3	6.3	16.1	9.7	7.2	1.8
Sverdlovsk oblast	3,440.4	63.7	59.5	4.9	11.7	14.2	5.4	1.4
Komi-Permvak aut. okrug	102.1	69.2	53.3	8.5	23.7	5.4	3.0	2.1

Taimyr aut. okrug	28.9	65.6	49.7	10.1	12.1	15.0	6.5	2.0
Khanty-Mansi aut. okrug	827.6	62.4	52.5	7.6	12.8	15.1	6.6	1.4
Yamal-Nenets aut. okrug	296.7	63.7	55.3	7.6	9.2	15.8	6.3	1.4
Urals-Siberia	6,715.7	64.5	57.0	5.8	13.3	12.8	6.1	1.5
Altay	130.6	74.1	28.5	4.8	43.6	13.0	3.5	1.6
Buryatia	688.5	64.0	30.6	4.8	40.2	10.6	7.6	1.4
Khakassia	393.7	65.8	29.2	9.7	35.2	12.5	7.2	1.6
Altayskiy kray	1,950.2	70.7	21.8	7.4	42.0	19.4	5.1	1.3
Amur oblast	697.5	68.6	26.6	7.9	41.9	11.8	6.1	2.1
Kemerovo oblast	2,167.3	66.6	23.0	11.6	38.9	15.3	5.3	1.6
Kurgan oblast	786.5	74.0	29.3	10.0	37.5	11.1	6.6	2.1
Novosibirsk oblast	2,036.4	71.2	25.6	9.8	35.0	10.0	13.9	1.7
Omsk oblast	1,528.1	73.8	32.8	6.9	37.0	8.4	9.0	2.1
Orenburg oblast	1,582.8	70.3	26.0	7.5	42.1	13.6	5.8	1.3
Chita oblast	823.3	64.4	24.5	12.9	39.1	11.7	5.5	2.1
Jewish aut. oblast	140.6	67.6	30.4	8.0	32.8	15.3	6.5	2.4
Aginskoye Buryat aut. okrug	44.2	69.1	44.7	5.7	35.7	5.3	2.6	1.3
Ust-OrdaBuryataut. okrug	82.9	71.1	37.0	4.6	40.0	8.5	4.0	1.4
Southern Siberia	13,052.7	69.6	26.3	8.8	38.9	12.9	7.4	1.7
Karelia	577.1	67.7	42.4	8.5	17.0	12.0	14.3	1.9
Komi	799.9	62.5	40.5	9.8	16.3	18.2	9.4	1.8
Arkhangelsk oblast	1,056.5	66.8	40.8	6.6	18.3	17.3	10.8	2.0
Vologda oblast	983.5	69.0	45.2	7.1	18.7	17.6	5.9	2.2
Murmansk oblast	788.0	59.6	40.6	7.0	12.1	25.4	9.7	2.0
Nenets aut. okrug	29.1	72.8	42.6	9.9	18.4	12.0	7.6	3.5
European North	4,234.1	65.3	42.0	7.7	16.8	18.1	9.6	2.0

Appendix 2 *(continued)*

Macroregions and regions	Number of voters, thousands	Turnout, %	VOTERS FOR					Voters against all candidates
			Yeltsin	*Zhirinovsky*	*Zyuganov*	*Lebed*	*Yavlinskiy*	
Bashkortostan	2,846.1	79.0	34.2	2.9	41.9	8.9	6.8	1.4
Tatarstan	2,635.8	73.7	38.3	2.6	38.1	7.4	6.9	1.6
Udmurtia	1,152.0	64.1	36.8	6.0	30.5	11.5	9.2	2.0
Samara oblast	2,459.1	69.8	36.1	5.6	35.2	11.6	6.2	1.6
Volga-Urals	9,093.0	73.1	36.2	3.8	37.8	9.5	6.9	1.6
Krasnodar kray	3,868.0	67.2	26.3	6.4	39.4	17.5	6.4	1.2
Stavropol kray	1,862.8	73.7	22.0	6.2	43.9	19.3	4.1	1.2
Astrakhan oblast	734.5	69.3	29.5	7.2	36.5	16.1	6.0	1.4
Volgograd oblast	2,003.8	71.9	28.6	6.6	40.0	13.6	6.4	1.4
Rostov oblast	3,301.3	75.6	29.1	4.6	35.0	20.0	7.7	1.1
Saratov oblast	2,045.8	73.5	28.4	7.1	41.6	12.8	5.3	1.7
Ulyanovsk oblast	1,090.3	71.1	23.8	7.4	45.8	12.3	5.9	1.5
Cossack South	14,906.5	71.8	27.0	6.2	39.7	16.7	6.2	1.3
Mariy El	550.1	69.3	24.3	7.4	43.4	11.0	7.4	1.9
Mordovia	688.8	70.2	24.1	6.9	49.7	10.6	3.0	0.9
Chuvashia	959.4	67.2	20.6	4.2	53.9	7.7	4.6	1.1
Belgorod oblast	1,093.4	75.7	22.9	4.3	46.3	17.0	5.7	1.3
Bryansk oblast	1,110.3	72.2	26.2	5.1	49.6	11.6	3.5	1.3
Voronezh oblast	1,963.0	71.9	22.6	5.8	45.5	17.5	4.4	1.4
Kursk oblast	1,007.5	73.2	24.1	3.9	51.1	11.1	5.4	1.3
Lipetsk oblast	945.7	70.8	25.1	5.3	46.4	13.2	5.6	1.5
Oryol oblast	687.0	74.0	21.5	4.4	54.2	11.8	3.9	1.6

Penza oblast	1,166.1	74.9	20.8	5.3	50.6	12.1	6.9	1.4
Pskov oblast	649.0	75.6	24.8	10.2	30.4	23.6	7.0	1.4
Ryazan oblast	1,027.5	73.5	24.7	5.4	40.1	19.8	5.6	1.6
Smolensk oblast	885.4	72.9	22.0	8.3	44.6	15.9	5.1	1.4
Tambov oblast	976.8	70.8	20.9	6.1	52.3	11.7	4.6	1.4
Red Chernozem	13,709.9	72.4	23.1	5.7	47.2	14.2	5.1	1.4
Kaliningrad oblast	724.1	71.7	33.5	7.2	23.1	19.3	12.8	1.4
Leningrad oblast	1,329.0	70.0	37.5	4.3	23.2	18.1	11.6	1.7
Novgorod oblast	577.9	72.0	35.7	6.2	23.7	18.5	11.0	1.7
Northern West	2,631.1	70.9	36.0	5.5	23.3	18.5	11.8	1.6
Adygeia	338.4	67.0	20.0	5.1	51.5	14.0	5.3	1.1
Dagestan	1,172.9	68.9	28.5	1.1	63.2	1.3	1.7	0.5
Karachayevo-Cherkessia	293.0	72.5	25.8	2.5	55.4	8.8	3.1	0.8
Northern Ossetia	435.1	68.9	19.3	3.2	62.3	9.6	1.8	1.1
"Red" Caucasus	2,239.4	69.1	25.1	2.3	60.3	5.8	2.4	0.8
Ingushetia	114.6	70.0	46.3	1.7	24.5	2.2	15.2	1.9
Kabardino-Balkaria	507.2	73.8	43.8	1.4	37.3	9.8	3.4	0.8
Kalmykia	200.2	75.7	58.5	3.6	25.7	5.4	2.5	0.9
Chechnya	507.2	72.6	65.1	1.4	16.3	2.5	4.3	2.2
"Blue" Caucasus	1,329.3	73.3	54.3	1.8	26.5	5.8	4.5	1.4
Vladimir oblast	1,243.7	70.5	30.9	6.7	29.9	19.9	7.4	1.6
Ivanovo oblast	957.6	72.0	29.6	7.0	23.2	29.6	6.1	1.5
Kirov oblast	1,199.7	72.7	31.2	8.6	29.0	13.7	12.1	2.0
Kostroma oblast	596.6	73.6	28.0	7.6	28.6	23.3	7.8	1.6
Nizhniy Novgorod oblast	2,852.2	66.2	34.8	5.4	32.5	14.8	7.1	1.7
Tver oblast	1,256.1	74.2	32.1	5.5	33.6	17.1	7.0	1.8
Kaluga oblast	833.0	72.9	31.4	5.1	35.4	15.6	7.5	1.5

Appendix 2 (continued)

Macroregions and regions	Number of voters, thousands	Turnout, %	VOTERS FOR						Voters against all candidates
			Yeltsin	Zhirinovsky	Zyuganov	Lebed	Yavlinsky	
Moscow oblast	5,385.1	70.5	44.2	3.0	24.1	15.1	7.9	1.7
Tula oblast	1,440.3	72.1	30.0	4.6	30.2	24.0	6.6	1.5
Yaroslavl oblast	1098.2	72.1	32.9	4.8	18.2	31.0	8.3	1.6
Non-Chernozem	16,862.4	70.8	35.8	5.0	27.8	18.4	7.8	1.7
Moscow City	6,784.9	68.9	61.2	1.5	14.9	9.6	8.0	1.5
St. Petersburg City	3,695.0	62.1	49.6	2.1	14.9	14.0	15.2	1.1
Capitals	10,479.9	66.5	57.4	1.7	14.9	11.1	10.3	1.3
Tuva	170.7	68.4	59.9	3.0	21.2	4.5	4.2	1.0
RUSSIA TOTAL	108,495.0	69.7	35.3	5.7	32.0	14.5	7.3	1.5

Appendix 3 Types of Voting in the First Round

Types of Regions	No. of Regions	NO. OF VOTERS			VOTES FOR CANDIDATES, %					VOTES FOR B. YELTSIN		VOTES FOR G. ZYUGANOV	
		No. (000)	Share of Total, %	Turn-out, %	B. Yeltsin	G. Zyu-ganov	A. Lebed	G. Yav-linskiy	V. Zhiri-novskiy	No. (000)	Share of Total, %	No. (000)	Share of Total, %
I. Dominance of B. Yeltsin	25	29,826.7	28.1	66.8	51.3	17.5	13.2	8.5	4.2	10,222.5	39.5	3,477.8	14.7
II. Yeltsin-Zyuganov, Lebed	7	6,469.9	6.1	69.8	36.1	23.4	19.2	10.5	5.9	1,629.7	6.3	1,057.9	4.5
III. Dominance of G. Zyuganov	28	32,848.5	30.9	70.7	24.2	44.9	14.4	5.2	6.5	5,629.3	21.7	10,432.0	44.2
IV. Yeltsin, Zyuganov-Lebed	11	14,640.9	13.8	69.8	32.7	33.0	16.3	7.2	5.8	3,344.7	12.9	3,379.2	14.3
V. Yeltsin, Zyuganov, Lebed	5	4,727.6	4.5	72.8	29.6	25.9	26.6	7.1	6.3	1,018.0	3.9	889.7	3.8
VI. Yeltsin, Zyuganov-Lebed, Yavlinskiy/ Zhirinivskiy	13	16,963.3	16.0	72.0	32.1	35.0	11.5	8.9	6.7	3,921.3	15.1	4,271.9	18.1
RUSSIA TOTAL	89	106,177.5	100.0	69.6	35.0	31.9	14.7	7.4	5.8	25,886.0	100.0	23,612.9	100.0

Appendix 4   Results of the Second Round, July 3, 1996

Regions	Number of voters, thousands	Turnout, %	VOTES FOR		Votes against all, thousands	VOTES FOR		Votes against all, %
			Yeltsin, thousands	Zyuganov, thousands		Yeltsin, %	Zyuganov, %	
Adygeia	340.5	64.9	76.1	133.7	7.6	34.5	60.5	3.4
Altay	131.1	70.9	40.0	48.1	3.5	43.0	51.7	3.8
Bashkortostan	2,851.3	80.5	1,170.8	990.1	83.5	51.0	43.1	3.6
Buryatia	689.9	61.7	192.9	210.8	16.0	45.3	49.5	3.8
Dagestan	1,208.3	72.9	471.2	401.1	7.4	53.5	45.5	0.8
Ingushetia	113.8	83.4	75.8	14.7	3.1	79.8	15.5	3.3
Kabardino-Balkaria	513.1	79.5	259.3	135.3	3.0	63.6	33.2	2.0
Kalmykia	200.8	73.4	103.5	39.4	2.9	70.3	26.7	2.0
Karachayevo-Cherkessia	296.3	74.2	109.7	101.4	5.3	49.9	46.1	2.4
Kareiia	580.9	65.3	251.2	100.1	25.0	66.2	26.4	6.6
Komi	791.8	60.5	308.3	134.2	31.6	64.4	28.0	6.6
Mariy El	550.7	68.8	154.3	199.9	19.6	40.7	52.5	5.2
Mordovia	692.9	75.4	238.4	249.5	16.3	45.6	47.7	3.1
Northern Ossetia	441.6	70.4	133.7	164.3	7.3	43.0	52.8	2.4
Sakha (Yakutia)	601.3	70.6	274.6	126.9	17.3	64.6	29.9	4.1
Tatarstan	2,632.4	77.5	1,253.1	658.8	74.2	61.5	32.3	3.6
Tuva	171.7	67.5	73.1	37.2	2.4	63.1	32.1	2.1
Udmurtia	1,156.1	64.3	392.6	302.6	40.3	52.8	40.7	5.4
Khakassia	396.3	62.4	116.7	116.6	11.8	47.2	47.1	4.8
Cechnya	503.7	74.5	275.5	80.9	15.2	73.4	21.5	4.0
Chuvashia	962.3	67.3	206.0	405.1	21.6	31.8	62.6	3.3
Altayskiy kray	1,953.6	67.1	505.3	727.5	65.0	38.6	55.5	3.0

Krasnodar kray	3,904.6	65.1	1,116.0	1,308.8	96.8	43.9	51.5	3.8
Krasnoyarsk kray	2,146.0	66.7	764.6	572.6	80.8	53.4	40.0	5.6
Primorskiy kray	1,586.1	63.3	524.4	395.5	74.2	52.3	39.4	7.4
Stavropol kray	1,871.0	71.6	548.7	722.9	56.3	40.9	53.9	4.2
Khaharovsk kray	1,106.0	66.1	430.9	246.4	47.8	59.0	33.7	6.5
Amur oblast	700.4	65.6	186.9	243.8	25.0	40.7	53.1	5.4
Arkhangelsk oblast	1,058.6	66.3	448.5	194.7	52.3	63.9	27.7	7.5
Astrakhan oblast	735.5	66.5	229.2	233.7	21.6	46.9	47.5	4.4
Belgorad oblast	1,098.9	75.4	300.5	485.0	33.9	36.3	58.6	4.1
Bryansk oblast	1,114.1	70.9	286.5	467.6	27.2	36.3	59.2	3.4
Vladimir oblast	1,250.5	65.3	421.4	342.1	46.1	51.6	41.9	5.6
Volgograd oblast	2,006.4	69.5	616.4	703.8	63.5	44.2	50.5	4.6
Vologda oblast	989.1	67.4	426.5	190.0	45.5	64.0	28.5	6.8
Voronezh oblast	1,968.9	68.8	501.1	781.3	62.0	37.0	57.6	4.6
Ivanovo oblast	957.3	68.6	349.4	256.6	45.4	53.2	39.1	6.9
Irkutsk oblast	1,802.8	61.0	578.5	437.1	69.1	52.6	39.5	6.3
Kaliningrad oblast	724.3	69.2	289.1	177.1	30.8	57.7	35.3	6.1
Kaluga oblast	839.3	71.3	290.6	272.6	29.8	48.6	45.6	5.0
Kamchatka oblast	274.8	58.7	99.7	47.6	12.8	61.8	29.5	8.0
Kemerovo oblast	2,169.6	63.0	567.8	704.3	80.1	41.5	51.5	5.9
Kirov oblast	1,201.2	69.9	425.5	348.8	56.9	50.7	41.5	6.8
Kostroma oblast	598.5	69.8	208.2	178.2	27.7	49.9	42.7	6.6
Kurgan oblast	786.5	72.1	246.1	284.7	30.7	43.4	50.2	5.4
Kursk oblast	1,010.4	70.5	258.2	419.8	24.7	36.2	58.9	3.5
Leningrad oblast	1,344.3	69.2	570.7	300.5	52.9	61.3	32.3	5.7
Lipetsk oblast	948.1	70.9	259.5	378.4	27.2	38.6	56.3	4.0
Magadan oblast	166.6	62.3	66.0	28.6	8.5	63.6	27.5	8.2
Moscow oblast	5,417.2	70.8	2,462.2	1,146.3	194.6	64.2	29.9	5.1

Appendix 4 *(continued)*

Regions	Number of voters, thousands	Turnout, %	VOTES FOR			VOTES FOR		
			Yeltsin, thousands	Zyuganov, thousands	Votes against all, thousands	Yeltsin, %	Zyuganov, %	Votes against all, %
Murmansk oblast	763.9	56.6	303.4	94.7	31.9	70.1	21.9	7.4
Nizhiny Novgorod oblast	2,860.9	65.3	967.3	791.7	91.3	51.7	42.4	4.9
Novgorod oblast	584.0	70.7	244.1	140.3	25.4	59.1	34.0	6.1
Novosibirsk oblast	2,039.8	66.9	596.6	666.9	85.7	43.7	48.9	6.3
Omsk oblast	1,526.0	72.9	514.4	528.6	57.2	46.2	47.5	5.1
Orenburg oblast	1,595.2	67.8	441.2	583.1	45.4	40.8	53.9	4.2
Oryol oblast	686.9	72.7	160.2	316.2	19.2	32.1	63.3	3.8
Penza oblast	1,168.5	72.3	299.8	497.8	38.7	35.5	58.9	4.6
Perm oblast	2,022.7	65.1	933.3	310.5	60.1	70.8	23.6	4.6
Pskov oblast	656.2	73.3	217.5	231.2	28.2	45.2	48.1	5.9
Rostov oblast	3,295.4	73.0	1,219.6	1,063.1	102.3	50.7	44.2	4.3
Ryazan oblast	1,031.5	71.3	313.1	379.6	36.2	42.6	51.6	4.9
Samara oblast	2,455.5	71.3	910.1	747.9	79.1	51.9	42.7	4.5
Saratov oblast	2,042.8	73.8	664.8	753.2	73.3	44.1	49.9	4.9
Sakhalin olast	461.1	62.1	152.8	111.1	19.6	53.4	38.8	6.8
Sverdlovsk oblast	3,452.3	65.0	1,726.5	401.5	98.6	76.9	17.9	4.4
Smolensk oblast	887.3	69.2	234.1	345.2	29.4	38.2	56.3	4.8
Tambovoblast	980.6	68.1	217.5	419.6	24.7	32.6	62.8	3.7
Tver oblast	1,268.5	71.6	455.7	396.6	49.9	50.2	43.7	5.5
Tomsk oblast	744.0	65.9	290.2	165.2	29.7	59.2	33.7	6.0
Tula oblast	1,440.5	71.1	536.8	421.2	54.9	52.4	41.1	5.4

Tyumen oblast	915.6	67.2	343.4	234.7	30.5	55.8	38.2	5.0
Ulyanovsk oblast	1,093.1	69.4	286.9	426.8	35.2	37.8	56.3	4.6
Chelyabinsk oblast	2,667.3	69.3	1,081.5	646.3	98.0	58.5	35.0	5.3
Chita oblast	827.4	62.0	209.8	269.4	27.3	40.9	52.5	5.3
Yaroslavl oblast	1,100.1	70.3	467.9	243.5	55.5	60.5	31.5	7.2
Moscow City	6,672.8	70.4	3,629.5	842.1	193.8	77.3	17.9	4.1
St. Petersburg City	3,659.5	65.1	1,760.0	502.5	112.7	73.9	21.1	4.7
Jewish aut. blast	141.5	65.5	45.8	40.5	5.3	49.4	43.7	5.8
Aginskoye Buryat aut. okrug	44.2	66.2	14.4	13.8	0.6	49.2	47.2	2.0
Korm Permyak aut. okrug	102.6	68.5	44.1	22.9	2.4	62.8	32.6	3.4
Koryak aut. okrug	21.9	67.9	10.4	3.4	0.9	69.8	22.9	6.2
Nenets aut. okrug	28.6	67.7	11.9	5.6	1.6	61.5	28.9	8.4
Taimyr aut. okrug	28.9	61.7	12.8	3.9	1.1	71.6	21.6	6.1
Ust-Ordynskiy aut. okrug	82.8	72.0	29.0	28.0	1.6	48.7	47.0	2.7
Khanty-Mansi aut. okrug	814.7	60.9	368.7	100.3	22.7	74.2	20.2	4.6
Chukotka aut. okrug	52.8	76.6	30.0	7.7	2.4	74.3	19.1	6.0
Evenk aut. okrug	12.9	62.4	5.3	2.3	0.4	65.8	28.3	5.1
Yamato-Nenets aut. okrug	271.9	66.1	142.5	27.3	8.5	79.3	15.2	4.7
RUSSIA TOTAL	108,600.7	68.8	40,208.4	30,113.3	3,604.6	53.8	40.3	4.8

Appendix 5 Dynamics of Yeltsin's and Zyuganov's Electorates by Region, 1991–1996

Regions	YELTSIN'S ELECTORATE (THOUSANDS)				ZYUGANOV'S ELECTORATE (THOUSANDS)			
	1991	1993	1995	1996	1991	1993	1995	1996
Adygeia	119.4	61.1	37.4	45.4	82.5	60.9	108.3	116.7
Altay	22.9	41.3	25.1	23.7	63.5	14.1	45.9	33.9
Bashkortostan	959.1	632.1	683.5	706.5	799.4	611.5	1,012.6	851.8
Buryatia	182.8	171.9	125.5	125.1	265.0	68.0	197.4	163.0
Dagestan	536.9	130.8	328.2	102.3	241.7	469.9	439.4	257.5
Ingushetia	—	49.9	48.7	29.3	—	4.1	5.5	16.3
Kabardino-Balkaria	236.1	141.9	140.8	158.3	102.3	90.6	151.7	134.1
Kalmykia	49.9	47.2	48.3	86.0	86.1	26.0	54.7	37.6
Karachayevo-Cherkessia	150.4	47.4	42.6	54.8	65.1	93.3	88.9	117.7
Kareiia	219.2	142.1	149.2	166.3	139.9	26.3	76.0	66.6
Komi	256.1	176.3	182.5	195.9	211.1	42.8	89.2	78.5
Mariy El	209.3	109.7	106.9	93.1	151.1	71.1	124.2	166.1
Mordovia	350.6	101.8	138.2	116.7	159.2	120.4	159.3	240.3
Northern Ossetia	101.4	172.1	152.2	210.5	215.7	67.3	124.9	83.6
Sakha (Yakutia)	234.9	78.1	45.2	57.8	233.4	93.7	157.8	187.0
Tatarstan	414.8	165.0	791.2	545.0	355.3	37.7	416.4	675.5
Tuva	19.2	58.6	58.7	70.0	94.3	11.3	29.5	24.7
Udmurtia	431.2	229.6	231.6	271.9	315.9	103.7	215.1	225.1
Khakassia	146.2	71.7	72.0	75.8	90.9	27.1	71.1	92.0
Cechnya	473.1	0.0	212.6	0.0	89.3	0.0	52.2	0.0
Chuvashia	376.5	182.2	97.9	132.4	266.2	160.0	262.9	347.5
Altayskiy kray	674.4	308.1	299.2	300.5	550.9	311.4	584.1	578.5
Krasnodar kray	1,157.5	664.7	488.1	682.6	951.7	434.5	809.6	1,024.6

Krasnoyarsk kray	917.8	391.4	427.5	523.1	412.9	167.1	384.1	428.7
Primorskiy kray	729.4	347.6	232.3	307.1	344.4	76.5	239.7	255.0
Stavropol kray	659.9	301.8	269.4	302.2	540.9	246.4	486.9	603.6
Khabarovsk kray	476.3	235.3	201.4	285.4	232.7	61.6	168.5	167.2
Amur oblast	201.1	145.9	105.2	127.2	260.4	90.7	205.7	200.2
Arkhangelsk oblast	446.8	262.8	270.1	278.1	262.8	64.2	148.5	120.2
Astrakhan oblast	303.6	139.2	147.2	146.4	182.1	92.2	148.3	183.4
Belgorod oblast	438.5	195.5	189.6	189.3	308.4	170.2	369.0	383.7
Bryansk oblast	479.2	223.5	168.9	208.8	296.8	198.5	336.3	396.6
Vladimir oblast	605.8	277.6	284.0	270.7	264.1	110.2	226.2	261.8
Volgograd oblast	789.4	332.9	334.7	411.7	419.3	247.2	475.6	576.4
Vologda oblast	412.4	205.4	238.5	306.2	257.8	105.9	155.9	126.3
Voronezh oblast	878.1	335.5	330.9	319.4	466.5	273.6	516.3	641.5
Ivanovo oblast	411.4	223.0	227.6	204.1	261.8	74.7	165.1	160.1
Irkutsk oblast	669.7	387.6	353.9	360.2	391.0	109.8	278.4	306.2
Kaliningrad oblast	202.4	152.5	149.0	173.8	206.8	45.8	115.2	119.8
Kaluga oblast	366.8	173.0	167.8	190.7	219.7	112.3	200.7	214.9
Kamchatka oblast	133.7	50.1	49.8	56.1	64.6	6.9	27.8	30.9
Kemerovo oblast	603.0	416.8	246.9	324.3	793.1	150.3	679.1	550.4
Kirov oblast	482.1	233.8	243.6	272.5	338.5	148.2	268.3	252.6
Kostroma oblast	241.5	136.2	129.0	121.1	185.3	70.5	138.9	123.0
Kurgan oblast	327.6	186.0	136.3	167.7	218.1	99.0	208.3	215.7
Kursk oblast	448.2	161.1	121.6	177.3	266.9	183.7	258.7	376.9
Leningrad oblast	459.6	247.5	294.2	348.5	328.9	78.0	241.0	215.5
Lipetsk oblast	459.0	169.1	137.4	168.1	198.0	133.6	242.1	310.7
Magadan oblast	78.6	33.9	32.2	38.7	55.2	5.7	16.9	16.7
Moscow oblast	2,520.9	1,179.4	1,297.5	1,675.4	1,040.0	396.0	945.9	912.7
Murmansk oblast	297.0	179.6	198.7	190.7	158.4	25.0	73.0	56.8

Appendix 5 (*continued*)

Regions	YELTSIN'S ELECTORATE (THOUSANDS)				ZYUGANOV'S ELECTORATE (THOUSANDS)			
	1991	1993	1995	1996	1991	1993	1995	1996
Nizhiny Novgorad oblast	1,504.4	546.7	556.3	658.0	490.0	264.2	493.9	614.5
Novgorad oblast	210.8	131.6	133.4	148.5	178.2	48.4	105.8	98.7
Novosibirsk oblast	835.8	324.3	372.5	362.3	449.8	175.0	423.9	483.4
Omsk oblast	625.0	340.7	281.1	360.0	336.0	167.3	356.4	403.3
Orenburg oblast	687.9	278.5	308.4	287.5	377.1	233.4	397.3	467.1
Oryol oblast	294.8	119.0	96.4	109.0	187.9	134.1	259.5	275.6
Penza oblast	588.8	192.0	160.5	181.8	262.8	200.7	405.6	442.1
Perm oblast	1,031.5	477.0	520.1	742.9	288.0	93.2	223.5	216.6
Pskov oblast	182.3	123.9	120.9	121.7	257.6	74.3	155.3	149.1
Rostov oblast	1,318.3	717.3	489.6	693.7	795.5	418.2	784.0	828.4
Ryazan oblast	438.4	219.9	172.6	186.5	288.4	147.4	307.0	302.5
Samara oblast	1,235.1	477.9	544.7	620.5	452.8	247.1	474.2	604.1
Saratov oblast	877.1	411.1	379.8	426.5	523.0	239.6	537.6	625.0
Sakhalin olast	189.3	83.9	73.6	86.8	112.2	21.2	82.0	78.8
Sverdlovsk oblast	2,282.0	805.2	892.2	1,303.0	240.7	143.0	301.4	255.5
Smolensk oblast	266.8	163.2	129.6	141.9	354.6	150.6	249.1	287.6
Tambov oblast	357.9	175.4	127.0	144.7	312.8	153.4	341.6	361.6
Tver oblast	446.3	273.5	250.2	299.4	424.7	184.3	342.7	313.2
Tomsk oblast	321.5	132.1	152.5	178.9	148.0	41.5	122.4	113.3
Tula oblast	725.4	307.2	291.6	310.2	295.8	144.3	309.1	313.4
Tyumen oblast	361.3	177.4	177.5	238.2	201.3	81.8	182.5	166.5
Ulyanovsk oblast	422.9	200.7	175.4	184.1	297.3	174.7	334.1	354.9

Chelyabinsk oblast	1,638.7	611.1	599.9	685.3	310.9	138.7	395.7	463.1
Chita oblast	232.8	142.6	127.2	129.4	301.9	67.6	196.5	206.0
Yaroslavl oblast	456.6	281.7	255.9	260.9	284.9	85.9	172.2	144.2
Moscow City	3,343.8	1,823.9	2,106.2	2,843.7	925.1	409.9	748.9	689.8
St. Petersburg City	1,659.9	776.5	959.6	1,137.4	569.6	154.4	409.2	342.5
Jewish aut. blast	44.4	28.4	25.0	28.9	46.6	9.9	33.9	21.2
Aginskoye Buryat aut. okrug	6.3	11.5	6.0	13.6	25.7	7.4	19.0	10.9
Korm Permyak aut. okrug	35.2	27.5	22.5	37.6	37.1	9.4	17.3	16.8
Koryak aut. okrug	8.8	5.8	5.5	7.2	8.4	1.0	2.3	2.4
Nenets aut. okrug	11.8	9.2	8.7	9.0	10.5	1.5	4.3	3.9
Taimyr aut. okrug	14.3	9.6	7.8	9.4	7.3	0.9	1.8	2.3
Ust-Ordynskiy aut. okrug	22.6	22.0	17.0	21.8	35.0	18.9	30.2	23.6
Khanty-Mansi aut. okrug	338.7	162.3	196.0	271.3	94.9	16.3	55.3	66.2
Chukotka aut. okrug	43.5	18.9	18.1	20.9	22.4	2.8	6.2	5.8
Evenk aut. okrug	4.4	3.9	3.0	3.7	4.7	0.8	1.6	1.7
Yamato-Nenets aut. okrug	127.9	70.2	90.2	104.5	36.7	6.1	16.0	17.4
RUSSIA TOTAL	45,552.0	21,618.9	23,394.3	25,886.0	24,502.1	10,877.8	22,501.9	23,612.9

Appendix 6   Dynamics of Yeltsin's and Zyuganov's Electorates by Macroregion, 1991–1996

Regions	YELTSIN'S ELECTORATE (THOUSANDS)				ZYUGANOV'S ELECTORATE (THOUSANDS)			
	1991	1993	1995	1996	1991	1993	1995	1996
North								
Kareiia	54.3	53.7	42.1	42.5	34.6	9.9	21.8	17.0
Komi	48.5	52.0	41.9	40.5	40.0	12.6	20.7	16.2
Arkhangelsk oblast	57.3	52.5	40.2	41.2	33.7	12.8	22.3	17.8
Vologda oblast	55.4	39.6	38.9	45.2	34.6	20.4	25.9	18.6
Murmansk oblast	56.7	50.1	41.7	40.6	30.2	7.0	15.7	12.1
Nenets aut. oblast	46.8	59.8	42.1	42.7	41.8	9.7	20.9	18.4
Northern West								
Kaliningrad oblast	41.0	44.7	33.4	33.5	41.9	13.4	26.1	23.1
Leningrasd oblast	51.0	39.7	36.0	37.5	36.7	12.5	29.9	23.2
Novograd oblast	47.8	43.9	36.2	35.7	40.4	16.2	29.1	23.7
Pskov oblast	34.3	30.8	26.1	24.8	48.5	18.4	33.9	30.4
St. Petersburg City	68.4	43.2	43.1	49.6	23.5	8.6	18.9	14.9
Center								
Bryansk oblast	54.7	34.9	22.3	26.2	33.9	31.0	44.7	49.7
Vladimir oblast	62.8	42.6	35.6	30.9	27.4	16.9	28.6	29.9
Ivanovo oblast	55.1	46.3	36.5	29.6	35.1	15.5	26.7	23.2
Kaluga oblast	55.7	37.7	30.9	31.4	33.4	24.4	37.2	35.4
Kostroma oblast	51.3	42.3	32.4	28.1	39.4	21.9	35.3	28.5
Moscow oblat	64.5	44.1	38.2	44.2	26.6	14.8	28.1	24.1
Oryol oblast	54.0	29.0	20.3	21.5	34.4	32.7	54.9	54.2
Ryazan oblast	53.5	36.7	24.6	24.7	35.2	24.6	44.0	40.1
Smolensk oblast	38.1	31.6	21.7	22.0	50.6	29.2	42.2	44.6

Tver oblast	44.3	39.1	29.0	32.1	42.2	26.3	40.0	33.6
Tula oblast	65.4	39.5	30.4	29.9	26.6	18.6	32.5	30.2
Yaroslavl oblast	55.6	51.3	34.9	32.9	34.7	15.6	24.4	18.2
Moscow City	73.9	55.4	48.5	61.2	20.4	12.5	17.5	14.8
Chernozem Center								
Belgorod oblast	51.2	30.0	23.5	22.9	36.0	26.1	46.0	46.3
Voronezh oblast	58.1	32.5	25.2	22.6	30.9	26.5	39.7	45.5
Kursk oblast	55.5	27.6	17.2	24.1	33.0	31.3	36.7	51.1
Lipetsk oblast	63.5	33.6	23.1	25.1	27.4	26.5	41.0	46.4
Tambov oblast	45.6	30.5	19.6	20.9	39.9	26.7	53.1	52.3
Volga-Vyatka								
Mariy El	52.7	41.2	29.6	24.3	38.0	26.7	34.7	43.4
Mordovia	62.9	26.4	30.9	24.1	28.6	31.2	35.9	49.7
Chuvashia	53.9	37.0	17.7	20.6	38.1	32.5	47.9	53.9
Kirov oblast	53.2	37.9	30.3	31.2	37.4	24.0	33.8	29.0
Nizhny Novgorod oblast	71.1	42.8	32.1	34.8	23.1	20.7	28.8	32.5
Volga								
Kalmykia	32.1	46.8	37.1	58.5	55.4	25.8	42.2	25.5
Tatarstan	46.6	50.4	51.7	33.5	39.9	11.5	27.4	41.6
Astrakhan oblast	57.6	43.0	33.0	29.3	34.5	28.5	33.4	36.8
Belgogord oblast	58.3	34.1	26.4	28.6	30.9	25.3	37.7	40.0
Penza oblast	63.0	28.6	19.9	20.8	28.1	29.9	50.4	50.6
Samara oblast	69.2	44.0	35.9	36.1	25.4	22.8	31.6	35.2
Saratov oblast	56.5	39.3	27.9	28.4	33.7	22.9	39.7	41.6
Ulyanovsk oblast	53.8	36.2	25.1	23.8	37.9	31.5	47.9	45.8
Northern Caucasus								
Adygeia	52.1	34.5	17.8	20.0	36.0	34.4	51.7	51.5
Dagestan	66.6	20.1	40.2	25.7	30.0	72.4	53.9	64.7

Appendix 6   (*continued*)

Regions	YELTSIN'S ELECTORATE (THOUSANDS)				ZYUGANOV'S ELECTORATE (THOUSANDS)			
	1991	*1993*	*1995*	*1996*	*1991*	*1993*	*1995*	*1996*
Ingushetia	—	86.0	78.1	44.9	—	7.1	8.9	25.0
Kabardino-Balkaria	64.7	51.6	41.6	43.9	28.0	33.0	45.1	37.2
Karachayevo-Cherkessia	62.7	25.1	24.5	25.8	27.2	49.4	51.3	55.4
Northern Ossetia	27.7	33.3	17.5	19.3	59.0	40.0	61.2	62.3
Chechnva*	77.5	—	71.1	—	14.6	—	17.8	—
Krasnodar kray	46.7	37.4	21.7	26.3	38.4	24.4	36.2	39.4
Stavropol kray	47.3	29.2	22.0	22.0	38.8	23.8	40.0	43.9
Rostov oblast	54.0	42.6	22.5	29.0	32.6	24.8	36.3	34.6
Urals								
Bashkortostan	48.4	41.2	33.5	34.3	40.3	39.8	49.9	41.3
Udmurtia	53.9	49.2	36.1	36.8	39.5	22.2	34.1	30.5
Kurgan oblast	54.1	45.1	25.5	29.2	36.0	24.0	39.2	37.6
Orenburg oblast	58.3	37.0	31.1	26.0	31.9	31.0	40.2	42.2
Perm oblast	73.2	60.3	45.4	55.3	20.4	11.8	19.9	16.1
Sverdlovsk oblast	85.6	54.9	50.4	59.5	9.0	9.8	17.3	11.7
Chelyabinsk oblast	78.2	50.9	37.0	36.6	14.8	11.5	24.6	24.7
Komi-Permyak aut. okru	42.5	55.5	36.6	53.3	44.8	19.0	28.6	23.7
Western Siberia								
Altay	23.1	57.7	26.8	29.2	64.2	19.8	49.1	41.6
Altayskiy kray	47.4	32.9	23.3	21.8	38.8	33.3	45.7	42.0
Kemerovo oblast	40.2	42.1	19.1	23.0	52.9	15.2	52.6	39.0
Novosibirsk oblast	58.6	37.3	28.3	25.9	31.5	20.1	32.4	34.5

Omsk oblast	54.1	45.7	28.2	32.9	29.1	22.5	35.9	36.8
Tomsk oblast	62.1	46.3	33.8	34.9	28.6	14.5	27.3	22.1
Tyumen oblast	57.2	46.8	32.8	39.1	31.9	21.6	34.1	27.3
Khanty-Mansi aut. okrug	69.5	56.5	44.5	52.5	19.5	5.7	12.9	12.8
Yamal-Nenets aut. okrug	68.7	58.9	49.0	55.3	19.7	5.1	9.2	9.2
Eastern Siberia								
Buryatia	35.2	53.2	29.8	30.5	51.1	21.0	47.5	39.8
Tuva	15.7	72.5	56.4	59.9	77.0	14.0	28.6	21.2
Khakassia	54.3	46.6	33.1	29.2	33.8	17.6	32.9	35.5
Krasnoyarsk kray	60.9	39.6	31.8	34.8	27.4	16.9	28.9	28.5
Irkutsk oblast	54.1	51.0	34.6	32.4	31.6	14.4	27.6	27.5
Chita oblast	37.6	42.1	25.2	24.6	48.7	19.9	39.3	39.1
Aginskoye Buryat aut. okrug	18.1	48.7	19.8	44.7	73.4	31.2	63.0	35.7
Tamyr aut. okrug	59.1	63.0	45.2	49.7	30.1	5.7	10.7	12.1
Ust-Ordynskoye aut. okrug	33.1	43.2	29.9	37.0	51.4	37.1	53.4	40.0
Evenk aut. okrug	39.5	55.8	37.8	43.4	42.1	11.0	21.3	20.0
Far East								
Sakha (Yakutia)	45.7	52.9	40.1	51.6	45.4	20.7	33.3	20.5
Primorskiy kray	62.4	51.2	24.7	29.6	29.4	11.3	25.7	24.5
Khabarovsk kray	60.7	53.1	29.1	39.1	29.6	13.9	24.7	22.9
Amur oblast	38.4	41.9	23.0	26.6	49.7	26.0	45.4	41.9
Kamchatka oblast	61.5	44.7	30.6	34.3	29.7	6.2	17.3	18.9
Magadan oblast	52.1	42.1	32.5	37.2	36.6	7.1	17.4	16.0
Sakhalin oblast	55.9	40.9	28.4	29.8	33.1	10.3	32.0	27.0
Jewish aut. oblast	43.5	49.3	28.6	30.4	45.6	17.3	39.1	32.8
Koryak aut. okrug	43.8	51.2	40.9	45.9	41.9	8.8	17.5	15.0
Chukotka aut. okrug	58.3	50.1	45.4	48.5	30.0	7.6	16.0	13.5
RUSSIA TOTAL	58.6	41.9	33.0	35.0	31.5	21.8	33.1	31.9

Appendix 7   Dynamics of Electoral Support for "Third" Candidates by Macroregion, 1991–1996

Regions	V. ZHIRINOVKSIY'S ELECTORATE				G. YAVLINSKIY'S ELECTORATE			S. FYODOROV'S ELECTORATE			A. LEBED'S ELECTORATE	
	1991[a]	1993[b]	1995[b]	1996[c]	1993[d]	1995[e]	1996[f]	1993[g]	1995[h]	1996[i]	1995[j]	1996[k]
North												
Kareiia	8.2	21.1	13.9	8.5	11.2	7.5	14.3	4.1	5.3	1.0	5.7	12.1
Komi	8.9	24.3	17.9	9.7	7.1	5.5	9.5	4.0	3.7	0.9	6.6	18.3
Arkhangelsk oblast	6.7	22.2	11.0	6.5	8.2	7.7	10.9	4.2	8.4	1.6	6.8	17.4
Vologda oblast	8.0	29.7	14.7	7.1	5.8	5.5	5.9	4.5	3.5	0.9	8.0	17.6
Murmansk oblast	10.0	24.3	12.6	7.0	14.3	10.6	9.7	4.4	5.3	0.9	10.0	25.4
Nenets aut. oblast	8.6	19.1	17.2	9.9	6.6	4.1	7.7	4.7	4.6	2.2	4.6	12.0
Northern West												
Kaliningrad oblast	13.6	30.0	11.6	7.2	7.9	8.2	12.8	3.9	4.9	0.6	12.5	19.3
Leningrasd oblast	9.2	30.0	8.2	4.3	13.4	8.2	11.6	4.4	4.9	1.2	9.7	18.1
Novograd oblast	9.6	29.6	12.4	6.3	7.6	7.4	11.0	2.7	3.7	8.8	8.2	18.5
Pskov oblast	15.1	43.0	21.1	10.2	5.6	4.9	7.0	2.1	4.2	0.7	7.3	23.6
St. Petersburg City	5.7	18.0	3.5	2.1	21.2	16.0	15.2	9.0	6.6	1.1	9.2	14.0
Center												
Bryansk oblast	9.6	27.2	20.1	5.1	4.5	2.4	3.5	2.5	2.6	0.6	5.9	11.5
Vladimir oblast	7.7	29.5	15.0	6.7	7.7	6.5	7.4	3.3	3.4	0.8	8.3	19.9
Ivanovo oblast	7.4	28.2	17.8	7.0	6.8	5.5	6.1	3.2	3.2	0.6	7.1	29.6
Kaluga oblast	8.7	28.1	10.3	5.1	7.0	5.3	7.5	2.9	3.8	0.9	9.9	15.6
Kostroma oblast	7.3	26.1	11.7	7.6	6.9	4.4	7.8	2.8	3.1	0.8	10.7	23.3
Moscow oblat	6.6	26.6	5.3	3.0	9.7	11.0	7.9	4.7	3.8	0.9	10.4	15.1
Oryol oblast	9.5	31.8	9.6	4.4	4.1	2.8	3.9	2.3	2.8	0.6	7.8	11.8
Ryazan oblast	9.1	30.8	11.0	5.4	5.7	4.2	3.6	2.2	2.6	0.7	11.3	19.8

Smolensk oblast	9.5	32.6	19.9	8.3	4.7	4.0	5.1	1.8	2.6	0.6	7.4	15.9
Tver oblast	11.1	25.5	7.3	5.5	6.0	5.6	7.0	3.1	3.2	0.7	12.3	17.1
Tula oblast	6.3	30.4	13.5	4.6	8.7	5.2	6.6	2.9	2.6	0.6	13.2	24.0
Yaroslavl oblast	7.3	21.7	10.1	4.8	7.3	11.7	8.3	4.0	3.4	0.6	12.2	31.0
Moscow City	4.1	12.8	2.6	1.5	12.1	14.9	8.0	7.2	4.5	0.8	9.1	9.6
Chernozem Center												
Belgorod oblast	10.7	37.1	14.8	4.3	4.6	3.8	5.7	2.2	2.2	0.5	7.7	17.0
Voronezh oblast	9.3	30.6	14.7	5.8	7.8	4.4	4.4	2.5	2.9	0.8	10.5	17.5
Kursk oblast	9.3	33.5	6.2	3.9	4.8	2.4	5.4	2.6	2.2	0.6	33.7	11.1
Lipetsk oblast	7.1	31.7	12.1	5.3	5.9	3.3	5.6	2.3	2.9	0.7	15.5	13.2
Tambov oblast	12.4	35.3	12.4	6.1	5.3	2.9	4.6	2.1	3.3	0.8	6.5	11.7
Volga-Vyatka												
Mariy El	6.7	24.5	21.1	7.4	4.5	2.8	7.4	3.1	3.6	1.3	5.3	11.0
Mordovia	7.1	35.3	20.1	6.9	5.4	2.4	3.0	1.7	1.9	0.7	7.7	10.6
Chuvashia	5.7	22.5	12.7	4.2	3.4	1.7	4.6	4.6	12.1	3.2	6.0	7.7
Kirov oblast	7.2	27.5	17.4	8.6	7.5	6.7	12.1	3.1	3.1	0.8	6.2	13.7
Nizhny Novgorod oblast	4.2	19.9	12.4	5.4	12.2	10.6	7.1	4.4	2.5	0.9	10.7	14.8
Volga												
Kalmykia	10.7	20.3	9.9	3.6	4.8	2.5	2.5	2.3	1.8	0.4	4.6	5.5
Tatarstan	9.7	22.0	5.0	2.9	11.6	4.1	7.1	4.6	3.5	1.0	5.1	7.6
Astrakhan oblast	5.8	17.2	16.7	7.2	7.9	4.0	6.0	3.3	3.9	0.9	6.8	16.1
Belgogord oblast	9.5	27.7	14.9	6.6	9.5	6.7	6.4	3.4	4.9	1.3	7.7	13.6
Penza oblast	7.2	32.6	11.2	5.3	7.0	6.0	6.9	2.0	3.0	0.7	7.5	12.1
Samara oblast	3.8	19.7	12.5	5.6	8.7	5.0	6.2	4.8	3.7	1.0	8.9	11.6
Saratov oblast	8.0	26.6	15.7	7.1	8.6	3.9	5.3	2.5	2.6	0.9	7.9	12.8
Ulyanovsk oblast	6.8	24.6	13.6	7.4	4.8	2.9	5.9	3.0	3.1	0.9	5.5	12.3
Northern Caucasus												
Adygeia	10.5	18.1	9.8	5.1	10.9	4.5	5.3	2.2	5.2	4.0	9.8	14.0
Dagestan	2.3	3.4	1.0	1.3	3.3	0.6	2.0	0.8	0.6	0.4	3.2	2.0

Appendix 7 (continued)

Regions	V. ZHIRINOVKSIY'S ELECTORATE				G. YAVLINSKIY'S ELECTORATE			S. FYODOROV'S ELECTORATE			A. LEBED'S ELECTORATE	
	1991[a]	1993[b]	1995[b]	1996[c]	1993[d]	1995[e]	1996[f]	1993[g]	1995[h]	1996[i]	1995[j]	1996[k]
Ingushetia	—	3.2	2.2	1.6	2.1	5.3	16.4	1.6	0.4	0.8	2.2	1.9
Kabardino-Balkaria	5.9	8.8	3.1	1.4	4.2	2.6	3.4	2.4	1.6	0.5	5.2	9.7
Karachayevo-Cherkessia	8.2	20.2	7.1	2.5	3.4	1.9	3.1	1.9	1.5	0.5	12.9	8.8
Northern Ossetia	11.3	17.5	10.4	3.2	5.0	1.5	1.8	4.2	2.0	0.6	6.0	9.6
Chechnya*	6.4	—	1.5	—	—	1.4	—	—	0.2	—	6.4	—
Krasnodar kray	13.1	25.5	15.4	6.4	9.5	6.4	6.4	3.2	4.5	0.9	14.1	7.5
Stavropol kray	12.3	38.5	13.2	6.2	5.1	3.1	4.1	3.3	3.5	0.8	16.5	19.3
Rostov oblast	11.7	22.3	10.4	4.6	7.4	14.1	7.8	2.9	3.5	0.6	11.3	20.3
Urals												
Bashkortostan	7.9	12.6	4.7	2.9	3.9	4.3	7.0	2.5	1.7	0.6	3.6	9.2
Udmurtia	4.4	17.6	9.7	6.0	8.2	4.4	9.2	2.9	3.0	0.9	9.9	11.5
Kurgan oblast	8.0	23.7	19.9	10.0	4.0	3.2	6.6	3.2	3.5	0.8	5.9	11.1
Orenburg oblast	8.3	22.5	12.0	7.5	5.9	4.0	5.9	3.5	2.9	0.9	7.9	13.6
Perm oblast	5.1	14.8	15.1	6.3	8.2	5.6	7.2	4.9	4.7	0.9	5.6	9.7
Sverdlovsk oblast	4.5	17.7	9.4	4.9	8.2	6.6	5.4	9.4	5.9	1.1	6.9	14.2
Chelyabinsk oblast	5.8	20.4	10.3	5.2	11.3	9.9	8.8	5.8	4.9	0.7	10.4	19.8
Komi-Permyak aut. okru	9.5	19.4	22.4	8.5	3.2	1.5	3.0	3.0	1.7	0.5	3.9	5.4
Western Siberia												
Altay	10.6	17.0	9.6	4.8	3.2	2.2	3.8	2.3	3.2	0.9	5.4	14.2
Altayskiy kray	11.9	27.7	15.8	7.4	3.2	3.6	5.1	2.9	3.6	0.7	5.9	19.4
Kemerovo oblast	5.9	29.4	12.9	11.7	6.8	2.9	5.3	6.5	7.2	1.6	3.4	15.2
Novosibirsk oblast	8.1	25.6	18.5	9.6	12.2	5.8	14.2	4.7	4.4	1.0	7.1	10.1

Omsk oblast	13.7	21.2	16.4	6.9	4.9	3.6	9.1	5.8	5.3	0.8	6.2	8.4
Tomsk oblast	7.0	21.9	10.8	7.1	11.8	10.4	10.9	5.4	3.6	0.8	10.8	19.7
Tyumen oblast	9.2	21.0	11.3	9.4	5.9	4.4	5.7	4.6	6.0	0.8	8.5	13.3
Khanty-Mansi aut. okrug	9.8	21.2	15.5	7.6	8.2	5.7	6.6	8.4	10.7	1.4	7.2	15.1
Yamal-Nenets aut. okrug	10.6	19.6	15.1	7.6	9.1	6.2	6.3	7.3	11.2	1.6	6.3	15.8
Eastern Siberia												
Buryatia	11.7	17.3	8.8	4.8	5.8	2.8	7.9	2.7	4.2	1.3	4.3	10.8
Tuva	5.6	9.7	5.7	3.0	2.1	1.4	4.2	1.7	1.6	0.5	2.6	4.5
Khakassia	10.2	27.4	14.6	9.7	3.9	4.0	7.2	4.5	3.8	1.2	8.5	12.5
Krasnoyarsk kray	9.9	31.2	12.8	7.6	7.3	6.9	10.0	5.0	3.8	0.9	12.4	13.9
Irkutsk oblast	12.8	21.5	15.9	8.4	6.7	6.6	8.9	6.4	6.1	2.0	6.5	16.3
Chita oblast	10.9	30.5	21.0	12.9	4.5	2.5	5.5	3.0	4.2	1.3	5.2	11.7
Aginskoye Buryat aut. okrug	6.3	14.4	9.2	5.7	4.0	1.2	2.6	1.7	1.6	0.8	2.8	5.3
Tamyr aut. okrug	9.1	17.4	15.6	10.1	7.9	6.1	6.5	6.1	6.9	1.5	9.0	15.0
Ust-Ordynskoye aut. okrug	13.2	14.4	7.3	4.6	2.1	2.0	4.0	3.2	2.2	1.1	2.7	8.5
Evenk aut. okrug	16.5	20.9	13.3	7.0	7.9	5.0	6.3	4.3	6.0	1.7	11.5	16.4
Far East												
Sakha (Yakutia)	6.8	15.4	7.0	3.6	7.0	3.6	4.7	3.9	3.9	1.1	6.7	13.0
Primorskiy kray	5.6	23.3	20.5	12.7	8.6	9.6	7.2	5.6	2.8	1.3	13.0	19.5
Khabarovsk kray	7.2	19.9	12.4	8.6	7.3	7.5	10.4	5.8	9.7	2.2	12.2	12.2
Amur oblast	9.2	24.9	13.1	7.9	4.7	3.4	6.1	2.5	3.1	1.2	9.2	11.8
Kamchatka oblast	5.4	27.2	16.3	9.8	17.6	20.4	17.4	4.3	4.0	1.0	6.8	14.1
Magadan oblast	9.3	29.2	22.5	10.8	16.5	7.6	6.0	5.1	6.9	1.4	8.8	24.0
Sakhalin oblast	8.3	36.9	15.6	9.0	7.6	6.8	9.3	4.2	5.6	1.4	7.9	18.7
Jewish aut. oblast	7.6	25.0	11.8	8.0	4.9	4.6	6.5	3.6	6.2	1.8	5.3	15.3
Koryak aut. okrug	11.1	24.1	13.6	6.5	11.9	9.4	9.0	4.0	5.7	1.3	6.1	15.8
Chukotka aut. okrug	9.6	23.3	13.5	7.6	12.2	6.5	6.4	6.7	6.8	2.0	6.6	17.1
RUSSIA TOTAL	8.0	24.4	11.4	5.8	7.8	6.9	7.4	4.1	4.1	0.9	8.9	14.7

[a] votes for V. Zhirinovskiy [b] votes for LDPR [c] votes for PST [d] votes for "Yavlinskiy-Boldyrev-Lukin" [e] votes for "Yabloko" [f] votes for G. Yavlinskiy [g] votes for RDDR [h] votes for S. Fyodorov [j] votes for KRO and nationalist parties, except for LDPR [k] votes for A. Lebed

Appendix 8 Correlation Matrix of Electoral Behavior, 1995–1996, for Eighty-nine Regions of Russia

	Votes for Yeltsin I (96)	Votes for Yeltsin II (96)	Votes for Zyuganov I (96)	Votes for Zyuganov II (96)	Votes for Zhirinovsky I (96)	Votes for Lebed' I (96)	Votes for Yavlinskiy I (96)	Turnout I (96)	Turnout II (96)	Turnout I (96)–II (96)	Turnout 95	Democrats	Center	Communists	"Women of Russia"	"Derzhava"	NDR	"Yabloko"	DVR	KPRF	KRO	LDPR	PST	Comm–USSR	APR	Winners' electoral base 95	Against all I (96)	Against all II (96)	Against all 95
Votes for Yeltsin I (96)	1.00																												
Votes for Yeltsin II (96)	0.90	1.00																											
Votes for Zyuganov I (96)	-0.77	-0.86	1.00																										
Votes for Zyuganov II (96)	-0.87	-0.99	0.90	1.00																									
Votes for Zhirinovsky I (96)	-0.22	-0.13	-0.23	0.05	1.00																								
Votes for Lebed' I (96)	-0.26	-0.02	-0.31	-0.06	0.35	1.00																							
Votes for Yavlinskiy I (96)	0.12	0.35	-0.50	-0.41	0.21	0.22	1.00																						
Turnout I (96)	-0.24	-0.33	0.39	0.36	-0.07	-0.28	-0.28	1.00																					
Turnout II (95)	-0.04	-0.08	0.35	0.13	-0.31	-0.24	-0.07	0.83	1.00																				
Turnout I (96)–II (96)	-0.28	-0.34	0.13	-0.05	0.45	0.01	-0.02	-0.24	-0.58	1.00																			
Turnout 95	-0.38	-0.49	0.45	0.49	-0.15	0.00	-0.29	0.76	0.51	-0.58	1.00																		
Democrats	0.32	0.53	-0.65	-0.58	0.16	0.40	0.66	-0.51	-0.46	0.40	-0.43	1.00																	
Center	0.77	0.76	-0.55	-0.73	-0.01	-0.29	0.16	-0.07	0.24	-0.29	-0.35	0.04	1.00																
Communists	-0.80	-0.92	0.84	0.93	0.11	0.07	-0.51	0.34	0.10	-0.43	0.52	-0.61	-0.81	1.00															
"Women of Russia"	0.32	0.36	-0.41	-0.41	0.27	0.44	0.36	0.10	0.31	0.43	-0.20	0.52	0.11	-0.32	1.00														
"Derzhava"	-0.23	-0.26	0.25	0.26	0.01	0.07	-0.30	-0.08	0.16	0.08	0.09	-0.20	-0.20	0.29	-0.21	1.00													
NDR	0.64	0.59	-0.30	-0.54	-0.39	-0.02	0.09	0.42	0.34	-0.62	0.16	0.90	-0.61	0.03	-0.51	0.11	1.00												
"Yabloko"	0.21	0.43	-0.56	-0.48	0.44	0.70	0.09	-0.29	-0.19	0.08	-0.20	0.03	-0.51	0.14	-0.09	-0.21	-0.06	1.00											
DVR	0.27	0.39	-0.24	-0.38	-0.01	0.31	0.31	-0.30	-0.27	0.16	-0.25	0.61	0.13	-0.43	-0.12	-0.09	0.09	0.40	1.00										
KPRF	-0.74	-0.79	0.88	0.81	-0.12	-0.01	-0.46	0.21	0.09	-0.39	0.40	-0.63	0.16	0.81	-0.39	0.16	-0.07	-0.41	-0.41	1.00									
KRO	-0.07	0.10	-0.24	-0.13	0.61	0.31	0.32	-0.07	-0.16	0.19	-0.16	0.39	0.19	-0.10	0.09	-0.07	-0.18	0.15	0.42	-0.16	1.00								
LDPR	-0.32	-0.27	-0.39	-0.05	0.36	0.21	-0.46	-0.15	-0.39	0.48	-0.02	-0.16	-0.38	0.25	-0.04	-0.09	-0.48	-0.34	0.07	-0.09	0.00	1.00							
PST	0.15	0.24	0.34	0.41	0.05	-0.11	0.10	0.11	0.60	-0.41	0.44	-0.30	-0.08	0.37	-0.15	0.44	-0.22	0.27	0.07	-0.27	0.17	0.23	1.00						
Comm–USSR	-0.28	-0.39	0.28	0.47	-0.14	-0.36	-0.37	0.25	-0.49	0.25	-0.08	-0.30	-0.15	0.37	-0.34	0.07	-0.22	-0.04	0.07	-0.27	-0.09	-0.08	-0.15	1.00					
APR	0.01	-0.22	0.26	0.26	0.00	0.25	0.31	0.18	0.46	-0.51	0.46	-0.51	-0.08	0.36	0.06	-0.05	-0.44	-0.29	-0.36	0.16	-0.08	-0.02	-0.08	0.39	1.00				
Winners' Electoral Base 95	-0.46	-0.45	0.58	0.58	-0.13	-0.37	-0.16	0.30	0.18	-0.44	0.27	-0.37	-0.20	0.41	-0.01	0.12	0.22	-0.13	-0.16	0.70	-0.13	0.04	-0.16	-0.01	-0.18	1.00			
Against all (96)	0.23	0.29	-0.52	-0.37	0.15	0.37	-0.16	-0.27	-0.10	0.27	-0.10	0.19	-0.11	-0.36	0.55	-0.11	-0.08	0.22	-0.13	-0.48	-0.04	0.34	0.23	-0.16	-0.24	-0.39	1.00		
Against all II (96)	-0.02	0.20	-0.57	-0.31	0.66	0.61	-0.27	-0.47	-0.16	0.53	-0.30	0.53	-0.07	-0.30	-0.08	-0.31	0.02	0.48	0.32	-0.42	0.48	-0.24	0.39	-0.43	-0.30	0.73	1.00	
Against all 95	0.46	0.51	-0.69	-0.56	0.18	0.33	-0.37	0.28	0.43	-0.20	0.43	-0.52	0.25	0.69	-0.21	-0.08	0.28	-0.01	-0.64	0.07	0.27	0.37	-0.16	0.07	-0.62	0.77	0.56	0.56	1.00

Appendix 9   Comparative Results of First- and Second- Round Turnout of the 1996 Presidential Elections

Regions	Voters I, thousands	Voters II, thousands	Voters I−II, thousands	Voters (II−I) *100/I	Turnout II, %	Turnout I, %	Turnout II−I, %	Turnout II−I, thousands
Karelia	580.9	577.1	3.8	0.66	65.3	67.7	−2.4	−11.5
Komi	791.8	799.9	−8.0	−1.01	60.5	62.5	−2.0	−21.0
Arkhangelsk oblast	1,058.6	1,056.5	2.0	0.19	66.3	66.8	−0.5	−3.9
Vologda oblast	989.1	983.5	5.6	0.57	67.4	69.0	−1.6	−12.1
Murmansk oblast	763.9	788.0	−24.1	−3.06	56.6	59.6	−3.0	−36.9
Nenets aut. okrug	28.6	29.1	−0.5	−1.69	67.7	72.8	−5.1	−1.8
North	4,212.9	4,234.1	−21.2	−0.50	63.6	65.3	−1.7	−87.3
Kaliningrad oblast	724.3	724.1	0.2	0.03	69.2	71.7	−2.5	−18.2
Leningrad oblast	1,344.3	1,329.0	15.2	1.15	69.2	70.0	−0.8	0.0
Novgorod oblast	584.0	577.9	6.1	1.06	70.7	72.0	−1.3	−3.4
Pskov oblast	656.2	649.0	7.2	1.12	73.3	75.6	−2.3	−9.6
St. Petersburg City	3,659.5	3,695.0	−35.5	−0.96	65.1	62.1	3.1	89.8
Northern West	6,968.4	6,975.0	−6.7	−0.10	67.6	66.7	0.9	58.6
Bryansk oblast	1,114.1	1,110.3	3.8	0.34	70.9	72.2	−1.3	−12.2
Vladimir oblast	1,250.5	1,243.7	6.8	0.55	65.3	70.5	−5.1	−59.3
Ivanovo oblast	957.3	957.6	−0.3	−0.03	68.6	72.0	−3.4	−32.6
Kaluga oblast	839.3	833.0	6.3	0.76	71.3	72.9	−1.6	−8.8
Kostroma oblast	598.5	596.6	1.9	0.32	69.8	73.6	−3.8	−21.4
Moscow oblast	5,417.2	5,385.1	32.2	0.60	70.8	70.5	0.3	40.4
Oryol oblast	686.9	687.0	−0.1	−0.01	72.7	74.0	−1.2	−8.4
Ryazan oblast	1,031.5	1,027.5	4.0	0.39	71.3	73.5	−2.2	−19.4

Appendix 9 (continued)

Regions	Voters I, thousands	Voters II, thousands	Voters I–II, thousands	Voters (II–I) *100/I	Turnout II, %	Turnout I, %	Turnout II–I, %	Turnout II–I, thousands
Smolensk oblast	887.3	885.4	1.9	0.21	69.2	72.9	−3.7	−31.6
Tver oblast	1,268.5	1,256.1	12.4	0.99	71.6	74.2	−2.6	−23.8
Tula oblast	1,440.5	1,440.3	0.2	0.02	71.1	72.1	−1.1	−15.1
Yaroslavl oblast	1,100.1	1,098.2	1.8	0.17	70.3	72.1	−1.9	−19.3
Moscow City	6,672.8	6,784.9	−112.1	−1.65	70.4	68.9	1.4	18.2
Center	23,264.5	23,305.6	−41.2	−0.18	70.3	71.0	−0.7	−193.4
Belgorod oblast	1,098.9	1,093.4	5.6	0.51	75.4	75.7	−0.4	0.3
Voronezh oblast	1,968.9	1,963.0	5.9	0.30	68.8	71.9	−3.0	−55.0
Kursk oblast	1,010.4	1,007.5	3.0	0.30	70.5	73.2	−2.7	−24.8
Lipetsk oblast	948.1	945.7	2.4	0.25	70.9	70.8	0.0	2.1
Tambov oblast	980.6	976.8	3.9	0.39	68.1	70.8	−2.7	−24.2
Chernozem Center	6,007.0	5,986.3	20.7	0.35	70.5	72.5	−1.9	−101.5
Mariy El	550.7	550.1	0.6	0.11	68.8	69.5	−0.8	−3.8
Mordovia	692.9	688.8	4.0	0.59	75.4	70.2	5.2	39.2
Chuvashia	962.3	959.4	2.9	0.30	67.3	67.2	0.1	2.9
Kirov oblast	1,201.2	1,199.7	1.5	0.13	69.9	72.7	−2.8	−33.1
Nizhny Novgorod oblast	2,860.9	2,852.2	8.7	0.31	65.3	66.2	−0.9	−19.6
Volga-Vyatka	6,268.0	6,250.2	17.8	0.28	67.9	68.3	−0.4	−14.4
Kalmykia	200.8	200.2	0.6	0.29	73.4	75.7	−2.3	−4.2
Tatarstan	2,632.4	2,635.8	−3.5	−0.13	77.5	73.7	3.7	95.7
Astrakhan oblast	735.5	734.5	1.0	0.13	66.5	69.3	−2.8	−19.7

Belgogord oblast	2,006.4	2,003.8	2.6	0.13	69.5	71.9	-2.4	-46.2
Penza oblast	1,168.5	1,166.1	2.4	0.21	72.3	74.9	-2.7	-29.3
Samara oblast	2,455.5	2,459.1	-3.6	-0.15	71.3	69.8	1.5	34.4
Saratov oblast	2,042.8	2,045.8	-3.0	-0.15	73.8	73.5	0.4	5.3
Ulyanovsk oblast	1,093.1	1,090.3	2.7	0.25	69.4	71.1	-1.7	-16.4
Volga	12,335.0	12,335.8	-0.7	-0.01	72.4	72.3	0.2	19.5
Adygeia	340.5	338.4	2.1	0.63	64.9	67.0	-2.1	-5.8
Dagestan	1,208.3	1,172.9	35.5	3.02	72.9	68.9	3.9	72.1
Ingushetia	113.8	114.6	-0.8	-0.66	83.4	70.0	13.4	14.7
Kabardino-Balkaria	513.1	507.2	5.9	1.17	79.5	73.8	5.6	33.2
Karachayevo-Cherkessia	296.3	293.0	3.3	1.13	74.2	72.5	1.8	7.6
Northern Ossetia	441.6	435.1	6.5	1.49	70.4	68.9	1.5	11.0
Chechnya*	503.7	507.2	-3.6	-0.70	74.5	72.6	1.9	6.9
Krasnodar kray	3,904.6	3,868.0	36.6	0.95	65.1	67.2	-2.1	-56.6
Stavropol kray	1,871.0	1,862.8	8.2	0.44	71.6	73.7	-2.1	-33.2
Rostov oblast	3,295.4	3,301.3	-5.8	-0.18	73.0	75.6	-2.6	-89.7
Northern Caucasus	12,488.5	12,400.5	87.9	0.71	70.5	71.3	-0.8	-39.8
Bashkortostan	2,851.3	2,846.1	5.3	0.19	80.5	79.0	1.5	45.7
Udmurtia	1,156.1	1,152.0	4.2	0.36	64.3	64.1	0.1	4.4
Kurgan oblast	786.5	786.5	0.0	0.00	72.1	74.0	-1.9	-15.2
Orenburg oblast	1,595.2	1,582.8	12.5	0.79	67.8	70.3	-2.5	-31.5
Perm oblast	2,022.7	2,020.0	2.6	0.13	65.1	66.6	-1.4	-27.0
Sverdlovsk oblast	3,452.3	3,440.4	12.0	0.35	65.0	63.7	1.3	52.9
Chelyabinsk oblast	2,667.3	2,663.8	3.5	0.13	69.3	70.3	-1.0	-23.6
Komi-Permyak aut. okrug	102.6	102.1	0.4	0.42	68.5	69.2	-0.6	-0.3
Urals	14,634.2	14,593.7	40.4	0.28	69.5	69.6	-0.2	5.3

Appendix 9 (continued)

Regions	Voters I, thousands	Voters II, thousands	Voters I–II, thousands	Voters (II–I) *100/I	Turnout II, %	Turnout I, %	Turnout II–I, %	Turnout II–I, thousands
Altay	131.1	130.6	0.5	0.37	70.9	74.1	−3.2	−3.8
Altayskiy kray	1,953.6	1,950.2	3.3	0.17	67.1	70.7	−3.6	−67.7
Kemerovo oblast	2,169.6	2,167.3	2.2	0.10	63.0	66.6	−3.6	−77.2
Novosibirsk oblast	2,039.8	2,036.4	3.4	0.17	66.9	71.2	−4.3	−85.7
Omsk oblast	1,526.0	1,528.1	−2.1	−0.14	72.9	73.8	−0.9	−14.9
Tomsk oblast	744.0	745.3	−1.3	−0.18	65.9	68.7	−2.8	−21.4
Tyumen oblast	915.6	907.8	7.8	0.86	67.2	67.2	0.0	5.6
Khanty-Mansi aut. okrug	814.7	827.6	−12.9	−1.56	60.9	62.4	−1.5	−20.0
Yamal-Nenets aut. okrug	271.9	296.7	−24.7	−8.34	66.1	63.7	2.4	−9.4
Western Siberia	10,566.2	10,590.1	−23.8	−0.23	66.5	69.1	−2.6	−294.5
Buryatia	689.9	688.5	1.5	0.21	61.7	64.0	−2.3	−14.9
Tuva	171.7	170.7	1.1	0.62	67.5	68.4	−0.9	−0.8
Khakassia	396.3	393.7	2.6	0.67	62.4	65.8	−3.4	−11.8
Krasnoyarsk kray	2,146.0	2,141.7	4.3	0.20	66.7	70.2	−3.5	−72.4
Irkutsk oblast	1,802.8	1,798.8	4.1	0.23	61.0	62.8	−1.8	−30.2
Chita oblast	827.4	823.3	4.1	0.50	62.0	64.4	−2.3	−16.8
Aginskoye Buryat aut. okrug	44.2	44.2	0.1	0.12	66.2	69.1	−2.8	−1.2
Taimyr aut. okrug	28.9	28.9	−0.0	−0.07	61.7	65.6	−3.8	−1.1
Ust-Ordynskoye aut. okrug	82.8	82.9	−0.1	−0.15	72.0	71.1	0.8	0.6
Evenk aut. okrug	12.9	12.9	−0.1	−0.62	62.4	65.5	−3.1	−0.5
Eastern Siberia	6,203.0	6,185.6	17.4	0.28	0.1	0.1	−0.0	−0.5

Sakha (Yakutia)	601.3	612.0	-10.7	-1.75	70.6	72.0	-1.3	-15.7
Primorskiy kray	1,586.1	1,580.0	6.1	0.39	63.3	66.1	-2.9	-41.4
Khabarovsk kray	1,106.0	1,103.9	2.1	0.19	66.1	67.0	-1.0	-9.2
Amur oblast	700.4	697.5	2.9	0.42	65.6	68.6	-3.0	-18.9
Kamchatka oblast	274.8	272.8	2.1	0.76	58.7	61.4	-2.7	-6.2
Magadan oblast	166.6	170.1	-3.4	-2.01	62.3	64.8	-2.5	-6.4
Sakhalin oblast	461.1	462.2	-1.1	-0.24	62.1	63.5	-1.4	-7.1
Jewish aut. oblast	141.5	140.6	0.8	0.59	65.5	67.6	-2.1	-2.4
Koryak aut. okrug	21.9	21.8	0.1	0.49	67.9	72.6	-4.7	-1.0
Chukotka aut. okrug	52.8	58.8	-6.1	-10.33	76.6	73.1	3.4	-2.6
Far East	5,112.5	5,119.7	-7.2	-11.5	64.9	67.0	-2.1	-110.9
RUSSIA TOTAL	108,600.7	108,495.0	105.7	0.10	68.8	69.7	-0.9	-880.5

Index

About the Author

Michael McFaul is an assistant professor of political science at Stanford University and a fellow at the Hoover Institution at Stanford specializing in economic and political reform in postcommunist countries. Before joining the Stanford faculty in 1995, he worked for two years as a senior associate for the Carnegie Endowment for International Peace in residence at the Carnegie Center in Moscow. He maintains his affiliation with the Moscow Carnegie Center and travels frequently to Russia, where he has lived for more than four years in the last decade. McFaul is also a research associate at the Center for International Security and Arms Control and a consultant to the Eurasia Foundation, the Agency for International Development, the Department of Defense, the National Democratic Institute, and CBS News.

McFaul was born and raised in Montana. He received his B.A. in international relations and Slavic languages and his M.A. in Slavic and East European studies from Stanford in 1986. He was awarded a Rhodes Scholarship to Oxford, where he completed his Ph.D. in international relations in 1991.

McFaul is the author and editor of several books including *Post-Communist Politics: Democratic Prospects in Russia and Eastern Europe* (Washington, D.C.: CSIS, 1993); with Sergei Markov, *The Troubled Birth of Russian Democracy: Political Parties, Programs and Profiles* (Stanford: Hoover Institution Press, 1993); and, with Tova Perlmutter, *Privatization, Conversion and Enterprise Reform in Russia* (Boulder, Colo.: Westview Press, 1995). His articles have appeared in *Foreign Affairs, Foreign Policy, International Organization, International Security, Journal of Democracy, Post-Soviet Affairs,* and *World Politics.*

McFaul also comments on current Russian and U.S.-Russian affairs, including articles in the *Chicago Tribune,* the *Los Angeles Times,* the *Moscow Times,* the *New Republic,* the *New York Times,* the *San Jose Mercury News,* the *Washington Post,* the *Washington Times,* and the *Weekly Standard* as well as television appearances on ABC, BBC, CBS, CNN, NBC, and PBS. During the 1995 parliamentary elections in Russia, he worked as senior consultant and commentator for CBS News. During the 1996 presidential election in Russia, he served as commentator for CNN. While in Moscow in 1994–1995, he coproduced and appeared in his own television program on democracy for the Russian Television Network.